# OLIVER PLUNKETT

Part I

Ireland's New Saint

by

Tomás Ó Fiaich

Part II

In His Own Words

by

Desmond Forristal

Our Sunday Visitor, Inc.
Huntington, Indiana

*Nihil Obstat:*
Kevin Kennedy, D.Hist., D.D.

*Imprimatur:*
✠Dermot
Archbishop of Dublin
August 27, 28, 1975

The *Nihil Obstat* and *Imprimatur* are a declaration that
a text is considered to be free of doctrinal or moral error.
They do not imply agreement with opinions expressed
by the authors.

First published 1975 by Veritas Publications. This edition published by arrangement with Veritas Publications, Booterstown Avenue, Co. Dublin.

ISBN: 0-87973-681-X

Library of Congress Catalog Card Number: 76-5978

Typography by Liam Miller
Cover design by Eric Neshiem

Published, printed and bound in the U.S.A. by
Our Sunday Visitor, Inc.
Noll Plaza
Huntington, Indiana 46750

681

# Contents

# Part I

## Oliver Plunkett
## Ireland's New Saint

Tomás Ó Fiaich

# 1  To Armagh via Rome

## Birth and upbringing

Oliver Plunkett was born at Loughcrew near Old-castle, Co. Meath, on 1 November 1625. His father, John Plunkett, owned a small estate of about 320 acres there and a further 360 acres in the neighbouring parishes until the Cromwellian confiscations. He was a kinsman of Lords Fingall, Dunsany and Louth. Through his mother, Thomasina Dillon, Oliver was a second cousin of the Earls of Roscommon and Fingall. He had an elder brother Edward and three younger sisters, Catherine, Anne and Mary. The future Primate was thus closely connected with the nobility of the Pale, but the oft-quoted letter claiming that he was descended on his father's side from the Earls of Fingall and on his mother's from the Earls of Roscommon is incorrect on both counts.

His first cousin once removed, the Cistercian Dr Patrick Plunkett, titular abbot of St Mary's Abbey, Dublin, and later successively Bishop of Ardagh and Meath, interested himself in the young lad's education and acted as his tutor from infancy until his sixteenth year. It is likely that Oliver spent part of this period in Killeen, the residence of Lord Fingall, where Dr Patrick was parish priest. He also spent part of it in

Dublin in the house of Sir Nicholas Plunkett, Dr Patrick's brother. He no doubt got an excellent grounding in the classics, the foundation of that familiarity with the Latin authors which he shows occasionally in his letters. He must have been on intimate terms with Dr Patrick's two famous brothers: Nicholas, who became Ireland's most distinguished lawyer, and Lucas, who was created first Earl of Fingall by King Charles I in 1628.

North-West Meath in Oliver's youth and for another two centuries was a mixed area linguistically, the meeting place of Gael and Gall. Though Oliver belonged to one of the most influential of the Anglo-Norman families, his upbringing around Loughcrew brought him into close contact with the Gaelic world further north. He must have become a fluent Irish speaker in his youth as he could still preach in that language on his return to Ireland after nearly a quarter of a century in Rome. Yet it is hardly likely that Oliver was author of either of the verses in Irish — one on the abandonment of Tara and the other on the decline in priestly standards — which are sometimes attributed to him in Irish manuscripts. All his surviving writings are in English, Latin or Italian. These were sent abroad and have survived in foreign archives. If he wrote also in Irish it was for his fellow Irishmen, and these writings have perished.

1641 saw the outbreak of the widespread Rising throughout Ulster which was destined to set all Ireland ablaze. From it came the efforts to unite

Gael and Pale in defence of their common Catholicism under the banner of the Confederation of Kilkenny. Over much of the country where the Catholic army held sway the church buildings were once again used for Catholic worship; bishops were consecrated, priests ordained and the Counter-Reformation promoted. But for Oliver Plunkett it brought also an interruption of his studies as Dr Patrick was a member of the Confederation and henceforward often absent in Kilkenny. Fr Peter Francis Scarampi, Papal Envoy to the Confederation, took an interest in the young lad and there are some indications that he made Oliver a member of his suite when travelling to various towns in Munster. When Oliver decided to study for the priesthood, Rome seemed the ideal spot for the further training of such a talented pupil.

## Journey to Rome

Fr Scarampi's return to Rome early in 1647 provided a good opportunity for Oliver to travel to Rome in his entourage. Along with John Brenan of Kilkenny who was to become Oliver's life-long friend and fellow bishop, and Peter Walshe who was destined to join Scarampi's own Oratorian order, Oliver Plunkett sailed from Waterford for Flanders in February 1647. A strong south wind had held up their departure for nearly two months. It is likely that two other Irish students accompanied them, James Stafford of Wexford and perhaps Robert Strange.

They were no sooner out in the open sea than they were pursued by two English warships. Fr Scarampi knelt on the deck of his vessel and vowed to his patron, St Francis, that if they escaped they would make a pilgrimage of thanksgiving to Assisi. A storm blew up and for two days their frail craft was buffeted by mountainous seas. When fair weather returned the enemy frigates were nowhere to be seen, and Fr Scarampi re-baptised their sturdy vessel the *Saint Francis* in gratitude to his patron.

A journey across Europe was a hazardous undertaking in 1647. The Thirty Years War had devastated a large part of Flanders and the German states; many contingents of the Spanish army, in arrears with their pay, lived off the countryside; bands of robbers roamed the rural areas. It was not surprising that the little Irish group soon found themselves prisoners, and secured their liberty only on payment of a large ransom.

From Flanders they made their way into France and arrived in Paris during the latter part of March. By early April they had reached Lyons but the most trying part of the journey was still ahead. Whether they continued overland through one of the passes across the Alps, as Hugh O'Neill and his companions had done forty years earlier, or journeyed south from Lyons to some coast town such as Marseilles to take ship for an Italian port we do not know. More than three weeks were required for this last stage of the journey and this no doubt included the promised visit to Assisi. It was May 1647 when Oliver Plunkett reached the Eternal City.

## A Roman student

The Irish College in Rome for the training of secular priests had been founded by Fr Luke Wadding in 1628 with an annual grant provided by Cardinal Ludovisi. One of the six pupils who entered it in its first year was the Ulsterman, Terence O'Kelly, who was destined to be one of the thorns in Oliver Plunkett's side on his appointment as Archbishop of Armagh. Under the terms of Cardinal Ludovisi's will the college was transferred from the Franciscans to the Jesuits and it moved in 1639 to new quarters in the street which is still known as "Via degli Ibernesi". But the students did not take kindly to their new Jesuit masters, and appeals followed by counter-appeals had brought the affairs of the college almost to a standstill by 1647. When Oliver Plunkett arrived in Rome, he found it impossible to obtain a free place in the Irish College, and for a year Fr Scarampi had to pay the monthly pension of the young Irishmen. He supported Oliver for as much as three years.

1648 was a year which brought some consolations, however, to the student in exile. On 19 March 1648 his former teacher, Dr Patrick Plunkett, was consecrated Bishop of Ardagh. In the same spring Dr Patrick's brother, Nicholas Plunkett, arrived in Rome as envoy from the Confederation of Kilkenny and was created a Papal Knight by Pope Innocent X.

## Towards the priesthood

At least four years (1650-54) and perhaps six (1648-54) were spent by Oliver in the old house in the Via degli Ibernesi. The college rarely had more than eight students in residence, usually two from each of the Irish provinces. According to the regulations then in force they should be 18-20 years of age, of good Catholic parents, healthy, intelligent and pious. Student-priests were not accepted "on account of the inconveniences that follow", nor students who had relatives or friends already among the Roman clergy, a regulation that became necessary "for the peace of the college".

Like all new students Oliver began his course with an eight day retreat and made a general confession. He received his college uniform and handed over his secular dress. On the day fixed for the swearing of the missionary oath, he went to Holy Communion and received the traditional threefold welcome in the refectory. His old clothes were then sold and the proceeds put into the college funds. He was now officially a member of the college community, sworn to return to Ireland to work there as a priest.

Breakfast consisted of a quarter loaf and a glass of wine. Lunch included soup, a plate of meat and cheese, to which fruit was sometimes added. The evening meal was much the same as lunch, but meat was excluded from one or other of these meals at certain times. Holidays were very limited—fifteen days in September, which were spent on the college vineyard at Castelgandolfo, and three other days allotted to outings.

Like the other students in the house Oliver took his courses in the Jesuit university "il Collegio Romano", where he soon, according to the then rector of the Irish College, "ranked among the foremost in talent, diligence and progress". His professors included the illustrious historian Pallavicini. From the Collegio Romano he moved on later to the Collegio di Propaganda Fide.

"Propaganda, in a word, all Rome," Oliver wrote many years later, "is a great book : how many nations with their various customs are seen there. Poles, Germans, Spaniards, French, Indians, Turks, Ethiopians, Africans, Americans, are met with, and one learns with what judgment the varying opinions and conflicting interests of so many different nations are harmonised. . . . One treats with Cardinals and Prelates of great wisdom, well versed and experienced in spiritual matters, and in the temporal affairs of so many monarchs and princes; and it is impossible that a person of even moderate talent would not derive great profit, as well in knowledge as in experience . . . an education most fitting for missionaries, more than in any other college." Oliver was no doubt thinking back over his own period of nearly a quarter of a century in Rome, an outstanding era in the history of that great city.

There was the Jubilee of 1650—while he was still a student—which brought nearly a million pilgrims to Rome, including the royal convert, Queen Christina of Sweden. Bernini's colonnade was gradually taking shape around St Peter's Square. In the Piazza Navona, another of Bernini's masterpieces, the "Fountain of the Obelisk" was inaugurated on Corpus Christi 1651 and Rainaldi and Borromini began work on the Church of St Agnes in the following year.

Meanwhile Oliver Plunkett and two of his companions were drawing nearer, step by step, to the priesthood. They received Tonsure and Minor Orders in the Basilica of St John Lateran on 4 March 1651; they were ordained to the sub-diaconate in the same basilica on 20 December 1653. For many years the records of Oliver's ordination to diaconate and priesthood escaped Irish researchers, but they were finally discovered in 1958 through the foresight of Dr Dominic Conway, now Bishop of Elphin. Oliver was ordained deacon in the chapel of Propaganda Fide College, off the Piazza di Spagna, on 26 December 1653 and was ordained priest in the same chapel on 1 January 1654. In each case the ordaining prelate was very appropriately an Irishman—Bishop Anthony Mageoghegan of Clonmacnois.

## Scholar and professor

Students who entered one of the Irish colleges on the Continent during the penal times had to take an oath on entry to return to the mission in Ireland after ordination unless they were exempted from this by their superiors. When Oliver Plunkett was ordained in 1654 the Cromwellian persecution was at its height at home; accordingly, Oliver petitioned on 14 June 1654 that he should be permitted to remain in Rome, making it clear at the same time that he was prepared to go to Ireland whenever his superiors would so command. It is the earliest letter in his own name which still survives in Oliver's own hand, but written in Latin and not in that simple Italian style which he was to employ in hundreds of letters from Ireland to Rome in the future. He proposed to take up residence with the Oratorian Fathers of S. Gerolamo della Carità, and no doubt the Rector of the Irish College concurred in his request. Presumably it was during these years that he obtained his doctorate in Theology and Canon Law, although the record of his higher studies has not yet turned up in the Roman archives. Fr Scarampi's death in 1656 was a sad blow —his name should always be remembered in Ireland not only for his gallant services to the Irish Catholics but also for the large part he played in the academic and spiritual training of Oliver Plunkett.

In 1657 Dr Plunkett's expertise in theology had become so well known in Rome that he was appointed lecturer of Theology and, later, of Controversy in the Collegio di Propaganda Fide. He was also nominated as Consultor of the Sacred Congregation of the Index. For twelve years he lived the life of a Roman professor, mixing with the greatest scholars of the era and bringing with him later to Ireland very happy

memories of this era in his life. The profound love of
Rome awakened in these years coloured all his subsequent writings.

Two of his acquaintances were Cardinal Pallavicini,
the famous historian, and Cardinal Casanatti, Secretary of Propaganda Fide, about whom he wrote from
Ireland in 1676: "While Your Eminence was Secretary of Propaganda, I had the honour of enjoying
your erudite and learned conversation, in company
with His Eminence Cardinal Pallavicini, of happy
memory, and I must in sincerity declare that from
such conversation I derived great instruction. Of this
and of many other favours received from Your
Eminence, I, although in these remote parts of the
world, retain a lively recollection. . . ."

Another of his Roman friends was Mgr Odescalchi,
who in 1676 became Pope as Innocent XI. In reference to him Oliver wrote later from Ireland: "It
would be difficult to express with what spiritual consolation and joy the Catholics of this kingdom, lay
and ecclesiastic, have received the announcement of
the merited exaltation of our Holy Father to the
Chair of St Peter. . . . While professing Theology
and Controversy in the College of Propaganda for
many years, I had experience of the sanctity of our
Holy Father, and of the great esteem in which he
was held by all for wisdom, prudence and holiness."

During his years as professor, Oliver continued to
reside with the Oratorian Fathers in S. Gerolamo
della Carità, which had been founded by St Philip

Neri himself. His spare time was devoted to works of charity, especially to the care of the sick in the nearby hospital of Santo Spirito. "In the house itself and in the city," writes Marangoni, the distinguished Oratorian of the next generation, "he wholly devoted himself to devout exercises; frequently did he visit the sanctuaries steeped with the blood of so many martyrs and he ardently sighed for the opportunity of sacrificing himself for the salvation of his country-men. He moreover frequented the hospital of Santo Spirito and employed himself even in the most abject ministrations serving the poor sick to the edification and wonder of the official doctors and servants of that place."

In addition to his other duties Oliver Plunkett acted as Roman agent for several of the Irish bishops. It was natural that he should be willing to serve his old teacher, now Bishop of Ardagh, for whom he obtained a transfer to Meath. But Dr Peter Talbot, who was appointed Archbishop of Dublin at the beginning of 1669, also nominated him as agent for the province of Dublin. His work as Roman agent must have occupied much of his attention in 1669 as several controversial questions such as the Rinuccini censures, the case of Fr Peter Walsh and *l'Affaire Taaffe* were among the matters he had to deal with.

## Appointment to Armagh

In March 1669 Dr Edmund O'Reilly, Archbishop of Armagh, died at Saumur in France. Apart from a brief visit to Dublin in 1666, when he had been kept under house arrest, he had been in exile for the last eight years of his life, a pitiable figure wandering across France, Belgium and Italy, seventy years of age, weighed down by illness and denied permission by the Viceroy to return to die in his native land. The Primate's absence had exacerbated the factions among the Irish clergy and the diocese of Armagh itself was torn by dissensions. It was essential to appoint a new Primate without delay and several names were suggested by letters to Rome in May 1669.

The seventeenth century Jesuit theologian, Richard Arsdekin, who met Oliver in Louvain in November 1669, claims that during a discussion of the merits of the candidates Pope Clement IX made a dramatic intervention to choose Oliver Plunkett: "There is no reason to prolong discussion of uncertainties when we have something certain before our eyes. Here is a man of proven virtue, of consummate doctrine, of daily experience in the city of Rome, outstanding for all gifts, Oliver Plunkett; him I constitute by Apostolic authority Archbishop of Armagh and Primate of Ireland."

Arsdekin's account is no doubt substantially true, but we also know that Dr Plunkett submitted a written application for the vacant See. There is no need to be apologetic about it or to seek to explain it away by suggesting that it was done only at the urge of his superiors in Rome. Oliver's letter of petition still survives in his own hand but it is neither signed nor dated. It is a brief, straightforward letter, obviously dashed off by a man who wrote out of a sense of duty and made no attempt to marshal any arguments in his own favour.

## Opposition

The appointment of outsiders and especially of natives of the Pale to the See of Armagh had been strenuously resisted by the northern clergy during the early seventeenth century and the 1669 appointment was no exception. An agent of the Armagh clergy in Rome submitted a petition to the Holy Father asking that no outsider and especially no Meathman should be appointed and if a native son were not selected that the appointment should be deferred. Oliver Plunkett answered this in a long document pointing out that several outsiders had been appointed to Armagh in the past and that his family and himself had always been loyal to the crown.

That Oliver Plunkett, despite starting off with the double disadvantage of being an outsider and a Meathman, quickly gained the loyalty and affection of the northern clergy is a measure of the man's gentle rule and winning ways. Yet there can be no doubt that the northern suspicion of Palesmen, fanned by the dissensions of the Confederation of Kilkenny and by the Remonstrance controversy, left some of his later decisions open to misrepresentation and made it easier for some northerners to cooperate in the plot against him.

## Farewell to Rome

Oliver's dearest wish was to be consecrated in Rome but despite his petition it was decided that consecration in Flanders was less likely to give offence in London. Before leaving the Eternal City he handed over a small vineyard which he possessed near Castelgandolfo to the Irish College, together with some books and pictures. He petitioned the Holy Father for the gold cross containing a relic of the True Cross which had been donated to Armagh in 1648 by the Bishop of Sidonia but had remained in St Isidore's because of the persecution in Ireland. And he paid a last visit to his beloved poor in Santo Spirito, where the saintly Polish priest, Jerome Mieskow, bade him farewell with the prophetic words: "My Lord, you are now going to shed your blood for the Catholic faith." Oliver replied: "I am unworthy of such a favour but help me with your prayers that this desire of mine may be fulfilled."

## Across Europe

Oliver left Rome on the long hard road that was to lead ultimately to Tyburn in early September 1669. Even before he got out of Italy he had run into difficulties. At Bologna he discovered that plague had broken out at Basle and therefore he determined to avoid the normal route through Switzerland and to head north-east through the modern Austria and Southern Germany. The route he followed brought him along some of the most scenic roads of Europe, but for the seventeenth-century traveller on horseback and on foot wild mountainous terrain was scarcely an adequate compensation for an extra few hundred miles.

We can follow his journey accurately from city to city. Through the Brenner Pass to Innsbrück; on to Munich; through Augsburg, Nürnberg, Würzburg to Mainz; down the Rhine to Cologne. Because of the ravages of the Spanish soldiers in the modern Belgium he did not chance going overland from Cologne to Brussels. Instead he sailed in disguise down the Rhine to Holland. Near Rotterdam the Dutch skipper got drunk and the boat with its twenty-five passengers ran aground on a sandbank. They had to wait for the next tide to refloat it. For four nights Oliver slept on the bare boards, exposed to every wind. Then via Antwerp to Brussels where he arrived on 3 November, the feastday of St Malachy—the only previous Archbishop of Armagh to be canonised by Rome.

To his great disappointment he discovered that the Internuncio had just gone off on business to Liège and would not return for more than a week. Oliver availed himself of this free week to visit the Irish Franciscan College in Louvain. Perhaps he inspected there the altar-plate belonging to Armagh Cathedral which had been brought for safe keeping by Hugh O'Neill at the time of the Flight of the Earls.

## Consecration

The consecration was arranged to take place in Ghent on 23 November, the Feast of St Columban. On the previous day he arrived in Ghent accompanied by Dr Nicholas French, the exiled Bishop of Ferns, only to discover that the Bishop of Ghent was indisposed and the ceremony would have to be postponed for a week. Oliver was worried about the long delays, the mounting costs, the heavy expenses which the consecration would entail. He lets us share his feelings in a letter to Rome written in the midst of his worries:

> . . . it will be necessary to give fifty pieces of eight to the household of the Bishop of Ghent, besides the expenses of the Masters of Ceremonies, candles, little barrels of wine (which is rather dear here), altar-linen, sacristans etc. . . . . It will be necessary to treat the consecrating bishops, e.g. with a pair of silver candlesticks, a chalice and such things. So the Bishop of Ferns tells me. But I have thought of giving them something devotional from Rome and making that do. They do not think of the poverty of our country and our bishoprics, whose greatest and best reward is to suffer for Christ. . . . They are accustomed to consecration on a magnificent scale.

In the long run the illness of the Bishop of Ghent

proved a blessing in disguise. For when the consecration was finally carried out by the Bishop of Ghent on 1 December 1669, the First Sunday of Advent, neither the Bishop of Ypres nor the Bishop of Antwerp was able to act as co-consecrator and the Bishop of Ghent was assisted by the Provost and Dean of the Cathedral. The ceremony took place quietly, not in St Bavon's Cathedral but behind closed doors in the private chapel of the episcopal residence.

## Homecoming

The new Archbishop lost no time in setting out for his diocese. He left Ghent on 3 December but was held up in Ostend for twelve days awaiting a favourable wind for England. He sailed across the Channel on 14 December and arrived in London on 16 December 1669. On the following day he was received in audience by the Queen, Catherine of Braganza, to whom he was introduced by her Head Chaplain, Fr Philip Howard, O.P., brother of the Duke of Norfolk. Fr Howard brought him on a tour of London by carriage and he was visited by many London priests, including the Dean of the Chapter. It is a measure of the peculiar religious set-up of Restoration London that while King Charles was being forced by Parliament to implement the laws against Catholic priests, his Queen was a practising Catholic and protected many priests in Whitehall Palace itself. It is rather amusing that only a few weeks after King

Charles had written to his Irish Viceroy asking him to apprehend Oliver Plunkett, the Archbishop actually lodged secretly for ten days in Fr Howard's apartments in the royal palace.

Dr Plunkett spent almost three months of the winter in London. It turned out to be one of the most severe winters within living memory, when "the cold is so intense that the wine of Spain was frozen in my chalice. . . . A heavy fall of snow succeeded the frost, so that it is impossible to travel while this cold lasts." No doubt he performed numerous episcopal functions in London — confirmations, probably also ordinations — as other Irish bishops did secretly during the seventeenth century. In London also he first adopted the surname Browne, which was to stand him in good stead on his arrival in Ireland.

Oliver's journey homeward — apart from the months spent in London — had so far been a very trying one, and the final stages of it were no less difficult. It is better to let him give his own vivid description, set down on paper a few days after his arrival in Dublin :

I at length arrived in this city on Monday morning last and I may say that I suffered more from London to Holyhead (where I boarded a vessel) than during the remainder of the journey from Rome to London — severe cold, stormy winds and a heavy fall of snow; and then when a thaw set in, the rivers became so swollen that three times I was up to my knees in water in the carriage; I was detained ten days at Holyhead because of contrary winds and then after an interval of ten hours I arrived at this port, where the many welcomes and embraces of my friends have deadened the sorrow which lay heavy on me because of my departure from Rome.

After a ten hour crossing from Holyhead the new Irish Primate sailed into Ringsend at nine o'clock on the morning of Monday, 10 March 1670.

## "Sheep without a shepherd"

The population of Ireland in 1670 was probably well under one million. Oliver Plunkett himself informs us that in most rural areas Catholics were in a majority of twenty to one. Yet he stresses that in the towns of his own diocese such as Drogheda, Dundalk, Ardee, Armagh and Dungannon, Protestants were in the majority and that certain areas of the north of Ireland were almost exclusively populated by Presbyterians.

Through the Cromwellian confiscations of the 1650s the vast majority of Catholic landowners east of the Shannon had been deprived of their lands. While a minority had recovered at least part of their estates after the Restoration of 1660, only three Catholic landowners had been restored in the whole of Ulster: the Earl of Antrim, Sir Henry O'Neill, and one of the Maginnesses. The descendants of the ancient nobility of Ulster were reduced to the status of tenants-at-will on a corner of their ancestral lands. Some, more vigorous than the rest, had enlisted in the armies of Spain or France; a small number had taken to the hills as Tories and lived dangerously, preying on the possessions of their new masters.

Since the church buildings were in the hands of

the Established Church and were in many cases in use for Protestant worship, the Catholics found themselves faced with the necessity of erecting chapels and Mass-houses insofar as the local authorities would tolerate these. Some of the cities and towns such as Dublin, Galway, Drogheda, etc. had already furnished themselves with reasonably appointed Mass-houses by the time of Oliver's return to Ireland—he pays tribute, for instance, to the fine chapels which the Capuchins, Jesuits and Franciscans then had in Drogheda, though the Augustinian one was much poorer. In the northern part of his diocese Catholic chapels and Mass-houses seem to have been extremely rare and Mass in the open air was the normal pattern of community worship.

## The Catholic clergy

Providing for the spiritual needs of the Catholic population was a body of about one thousand secular priests and upwards of six hundred regulars. Among the latter the Franciscans were by far the most numerous, having as many members as all the other orders together. Hundreds of priests, both secular and regular, had remained at their posts during the worst period of the Cromwellian persecution; the number had been increased considerably during the 1660s by the return of many priests from exile, the arrival of newly-ordained ones from the Continental colleges and the possibility once more of carrying out ordinations at home.

For a short period at the end of the 1660s the only
active Catholic bishop in Ireland was Dr Patrick
Plunkett, Bishop of Ardagh, Oliver's former tutor.
1669 saw, however, not only his transfer to Meath
and the appointment of Oliver to Armagh, but also
the filling of the other three archiepiscopal Sees with
the nominations of Peter Talbot to Dublin, William
Burgatt to Cashel and James Lynch to Tuam. In
addition, James Phelan was appointed Bishop of
Ossory. The other dioceses were governed by Vicars,
some appointed by Rome (Vicars Apostolic), some
appointed by the surviving members of the local
chapter (Vicars Capitular), some appointed by an
earlier bishop of the diocese or by the metropolitan
or by the senior suffragan bishop of the province
(Vicars General). In the absence of a clearly con-
stituted authority it is not surprising that disputes
about jurisdiction were frequent and acrimonious.

There were, unfortunately, several other issues
which had provoked serious dissensions among the
Irish clergy during the 1660s. Probably the most
serious was the Remonstrance, a declaration of loyalty
to the Crown containing several anti-Papal statements
which was vigorously promoted by Fr Peter Walsh
with the active support of the Viceroy Ormonde.
In an effort to settle the Remonstrance controversy
Rome despatched another Franciscan, Fr James
Taaffe, to Ireland in 1668 with very wide powers,
but the latter's indiscreet methods of procedure only
inflamed the dissensions. There were, too, contro-

versies at local level between seculars and regulars
concerning their respective rights, and between the
Franciscans and Dominicans concerning the right of
each group to quest for alms in certain areas of Ulster.

A decade of war during the 1640s followed by a
decade of active persecution of Catholicism in the
1650s meant that many of those ordained during this
period had been given very little in the way of formal
training for the priesthood. Most dioceses and orders
had a few men who were not amenable to discipline.
The absence of Catholic schools throughout most of
Ireland left the standard of education low among
the clergy. This was particularly true of the northern
dioceses, each of which had only a few priests who
had studied on the Continent. The late seventeenth-
century composition in Irish *Comhairle Mhic Clamha
ó Achadh na Muileann* provides a biting satire on the
ignorance, boorishness and ambition of a priest of
Oliver Plunkett's day. Even after allowing for exaggeration there can be no doubt that priests of the
"Mac Lave" type existed in the 1670s. The wonder is
that they were not more numerous, and that, given
the disadvantages outlined above, the vast majority
of Oliver's clergy still proved men of virtue, simple
piety and dedication to duty, who served their people
faithfully in the face of bitter persecution.

## A pastoral bishop

Oliver Plunkett was no sooner back in Ireland than
he threw himself into the reorganisation of the Church

with amazing energy. Both Sir Nicholas Plunkett and
the Earl of Fingall invited him to their residences,
as did also "three other knights who are married to
three of my cousins". But he was unwilling to spend
much time around Dublin or Meath, so anxious was
he to take up duty in his new diocese before the end
of Lent. The Baron of Louth had offered to provide
him with board and lodging there, not far from
Dundalk, and he felt that it would be a convenient
centre for diocesan administration. He was in time to
consecrate the Oils on Holy Thursday.

There is some evidence, however, that it was not
on the estate of Lord Louth but on the neighbouring
estate of Sir John Bellew that he took up residence
in the Dundalk area. He lodged for a period with
a certain Sylvester MacMahon (or Mathews) in the
townland of Haggardstown, just south of Dundalk.
This MacMahon family was well-to-do and members
of it leased land not only in Haggardstown but in
Ballybarrack, Rossmakea and other townlands of
North Louth. It was presumably under their protection that Dr Plunkett set up his little chapel in
Ballybarrack, and several ordinations were carried out
by him there and in Rossmakea. Shortly afterwards
a son of Sylvester Mathews named Andrew, who had
joined the Cistercian order, was ordained to the priesthood by Dr Plunkett and through the Archbishop's
influence was promoted to the position of titular abbot
of Mellifont. He served as parish priest of the united
parishes of Mellifont and Collon and on his death

the long line of Cistercian parish priests of these two parishes came to a sad end.

Within a short time of taking up residence near Dundalk Oliver Plunkett had convened two synods of the diocesan clergy: one possibly for the Co. Louth clergy in Pierce's Inn, Dunleer, and the other for the northern clergy in Blyke's Inn, Dorsey; he had held two ordination ceremonies and inside six weeks had confirmed more than ten thousand persons. Yet he estimated that, due to the lack of resident bishops during the previous decades, there were still fifty thousand people, many of them adults, to be confirmed throughout the northern province. During the spring he made himself fully acquainted with the affairs of the diocese so that he was able to send a very full report on it to Rome.

## Founder of schools

In Oliver's first report on the diocese of Armagh, compiled perhaps as early as April 1670, he emphasised the dangers to the faith inherent in the absence of Catholic schools: "The Catholics may not have schools and they are so poor since the war and subsequent exile of sixteen years under the tyrant Cromwell that they cannot keep schoolmasters in their homes and are thus compelled to send their children to Protestant schools." In a letter written to Rome around the same time he adverted to the need for further schooling among the young priests: "They know the Latin language well, but they are ignorant in moral theology and controversies. . . . If this country had the possibility of educating the sons of the Catholic gentlemen, what a noble and flourishing Church we would have."

While Oliver's initial impulse was to seek aid to send a few of his priests to Rome or Louvain, he quickly decided that the remedy must be provided at home. There it could serve the double purpose of training his priests and educating the Catholic youth. Even in these days of prefabricated school buildings it is amazing to learn that by the middle of July 1670 Oliver had "built from the foundations a commodious house, as also two schools where about 150 boys were educated and twenty-five ecclesiastics". Forty of the boys were the sons of Protestants, and the number of priests in attendance later rose to over fifty. With only a few exceptions the whole Armagh clergy must have gone back to school within the next few years.

The original location of the schools must have been in the Dundalk area, probably in the region of Ballybarrack. A number of Jesuit Fathers taught in them, the most notable being Fr Stephen Rice, who was later appointed superior of the Jesuits in Ireland. The only diocesan priest who served in them was Fr Edward Drumgoole who returned from Salamanca in 1671 and soon had "fifty-six priests in his class". Oliver provided everything for them, "even the frying-pan", out of his own meagre resources, spending more on them each year than his entire income from the archdiocese. By the summer of 1671 he had moved into residence with the Jesuit Fathers "near Dundalk" from a house which had been made available to him by a relative.

It was probably the continued expansion of the schools and the decision of Propaganda Fide to grant them financial assistance that induced Oliver to move them to Drogheda in 1672. The Jesuits had already a fine ornate chapel there and it was by far the largest town in the archdiocese. The assistance from Rome amounted to only 150 *scudi* (£37.50) per annum, and Oliver had to make great personal sacrifices to keep the schools open, dressing in cheap clothes and eating only the plainest fare.

The schools lasted three years and five months; they were levelled to the ground in November 1673 during the first outbreak of severe persecution which sent Oliver into hiding. Till the end of his life he was saddened by the remembrance of how this gallant achievement had been so suddenly shattered: "There is nothing that occasions me more inward grief than to see the schools instituted by me now destroyed after so many toils. Oh what will the Catholic youth do, which is both numerous and full of talent."

## Reformer of the clergy

Despite the sporadic outbursts of persecution the Irish Church in Oliver Plunkett's day was never faced with a serious shortage of priests. In fact the Primate was sometimes inclined to think that in the circum-

stances of the time there were too many priests and
he made this view known on occasions to the Holy
See:

> The secular clergy is too numerous; every gentle-
> man desires a chaplain and is anxious to hear Mass
> in his own room, under the pretence of fear of the
> government. They force the bishops to ordain priests
> and afterwards they turn the whole world upside
> down to procure a parish for this priest, their
> dependent.

Nevertheless the clergy were somewhat unevenly
distributed throughout the country. The diocese of
Meath, for example, had seventy parish priests, the
diocese of Raphoe had only fourteen to eighteen.
The number of priests in Oliver's own diocese of
Armagh is given in slightly different forms in his
various letters: "fifty parish priests or thereabouts"
in 1670, "fifty-six priests who serve my diocese" in
1671, "about forty parish priests" in 1675, "forty-two
pastors" in 1678. One gets the impression that the
figures given for 1671 and 1678 are exact figures for
these years. It seems reasonable to conclude, therefore,
that the Archbishop had always 40-42 parish priests
and 14-16 curates working in his archdiocese. We know
the names of the majority of these priests from various contemporary documents. Apart from a few sur-
vivors of the pre-Cromwellian era, they were all young
men, ordained in the 1660s by Bishop Patrick
Plunkett or in the 1670s by Oliver Plunkett himself.

Thirty-seven of them were still alive at the time of the 1704 Registration.

The clergy were supported by the free donations of the Catholic people and by stole fees. Each family gave two shillings per year to the parish priest, and in addition a shilling was paid on the occasion of a baptism and one-and-sixpence on the occasion of a marriage. The parish priests in turn contributed one pound each per annum to their bishop. On his arrival in Ireland Oliver was rather shocked to discover that a donation was requested on the occasion of conferring the sacraments, but he was soon convinced by the Bishop of Meath that it would be impossible for the clergy to live otherwise.

To build up a disciplined and educated clergy in Ireland after the havoc wrought by the Cromwellian era and to reform those who had gone astray was one of the great aims of Oliver's life as a bishop. "On my arrival in Ireland," he wrote later, "as the unworthy successor of St Patrick I regarded nothing as important as that I should set about the reformation of the clergy in the province of Armagh in order that they should be deeply imbued both with learning and with ecclesiastical discipline."

He was an ordaining bishop in the fullest sense of the term, holding ordinations regularly every single year up to and including the year of his arrest. As late as 1704 when the "Act for Registering the Popish Clergy" took effect and provided us with the names and ordination details of over a thousand priests throughout the country, there were 122 priests still surviving who had been ordained by the Archbishop. When one allows for deaths during the intervening quarter of a century and for the fact that hundreds of regulars had been forced abroad before 1704, the number of priests actually ordained by Oliver Plunkett must have totalled several hundred.

Taking the 1704 list as representative of his ordinations as a whole it may be deduced that the vast majority of the ordinations were carried out in Co. Louth and well over half of these took place at Ardpatrick. Ballybarrack figures as the most usual ordination site during his first couple of years in Ireland and Ardpatrick thereafter. Ordinations are also recorded for Rossmakea, Castletown, Haggardstown, Bridge, Dundalk and Louth, all in Co. Louth (the latter two may really refer to Ballybarrack and Ardpatrick respectively), for Iniskeen in Co. Monaghan, Derrycay in Co. Armagh, Emlock in Co. Meath, Dublin and Co. Cavan.

Besides ordaining so many priests at home in Ireland the Archbishop was always anxious that the benefits of a Continental education and especially of a Roman training should be made available to a number of his priests. He interested himself therefore in the affairs of the Irish colleges on the Continent and tried to break down the "closed shop" policy of the colleges in Bordeaux and Toulouse which catered only for students from Munster. The superior of the Jesuits in Ireland had the right to select the students for the Irish colleges in Spain and Portugal and the Primate tried to ensure that the selection would be made, not according to the part of Ireland to which the superior belonged, but on the basis of equality between all four provinces. In a letter to Propaganda Oliver provided a full list of the Irish colleges in Spain, Portugal, France and Belgium and called on the Cardinals to ensure that students from all parts of Ireland would be admitted to them without any discrimination. However, he always remained slightly suspicious of the training imparted outside Rome: "those who study in Paris come here with many ideas which do not please me", and he was always anxious to have some of his priests trained in Rome:

... I should like to select from among 150 scholars and priests whom I have in my school here a half dozen of the most intelligent and send them to Rome, so that the seed may remain in Israel. Here in Ireland I can give them an education of sorts in letters and cases of conscience, but in theology and controversies I cannot, nor can I prepare candidates fit for the episcopate or the office of vicar general, if I do not send them abroad; it is necessary that there be here some men with doctorates who can account for the things they believe. Little by little we shall be without the like, if we do not provide for their education and, as I said, the Roman education is the best. ...

Among the Roman colleges it was the Collegio di

Propaganda Fide rather than the Irish College which
had a particular attraction for him:

> . . . for the purpose of training a missionary there
> is not another college in the world more suitable
> than Propaganda, where for two hours in the morn-
> ing there are lectures in theology and in the after-
> noon one hour of controversies and then for a half
> hour or an hour cases of conscience; they learn to
> preach and they become masters of Hebrew and
> Greek; they officiate in Church and are trained in
> Gregorian Chant. Truly they have an education
> most fitting for missionaries, more so than in any
> other college. To tell the truth, they have not the
> like in the Irish College or the Scots College, where
> they study speculative questions about the prin-
> ciples of individuation, free terminations, *scientia
> media* and nothing else unless a man makes it his
> own private business to acquire positive learning.
> For this reason I fervently beseech you that I be
> allowed to send a half dozen of my most intelligent
> young priests to the said college, so that the pro-
> vince of Ulster may have men of knowledge with
> the ability to be leaders in their dioceses.

The Archbishop held such strong views on this
issue that he recommended that the buildings and
vineyard of the Irish College, Rome, should be sold
and the proceeds invested. If the interest, together
with the annual endowment of the college, were
handed over to Propaganda College, more than twice
as many Irish students could be maintained in the

latter as in the Irish college, with its separate buildings, three Jesuit Fathers and two servants. Perhaps
it was fortunate in the long run that his recommendation was not acted upon. To maintain a separate Irish
college in Rome in his day for six or eight students
may have seemed an uneconomic luxury, but he could
not have foreseen the flourishing college, *alma mater*
of a thousand Irish priests and *seminarium episco-
porum,* as it came to be called, which would one day
grow from it.

Oliver succeeded in having two places in Propaganda College reserved for students of the province
of Armagh (three from 1672 on). He was always on
the look-out for suitable candidates to send to Rome.
In the very first report which he compiled on the
diocese of Armagh he recommended that places in
Propaganda College should be provided for "two boys
of this most noble house" of O'Neill, one the son of
Sir Phelim and the other the son of Terence O'Neill,
"a gentleman accomplished in both peace and war".
The former, instead of going to Propaganda, entered
the Franciscan order, and became one of Oliver's
antagonists later. The other is probably identical with
the Niall O'Neill who, together with William Plunkett,
was sent by the Archbishop to study in Rome in
October 1671. Young O'Neill was already ill before
he reached Rome and he died during his student days
there before the summer of 1674. The Archbishop
then nominated Henry Dalton, who had studied
philosophy in Paris: "I am sending him to Rome

rather than to Paris to study theology, because it is in Rome that a better ecclesiastical education can be given and the theological formation given in Rome is based on sounder principles than that given in Paris. To tell the truth many of ours who come from Paris bring with them many ideas which I do not like."

In 1674 another young Armagh priest, Henry Hughes, was ordained in Rome and proceeded to his doctorate. After his return to Ireland Oliver appointed him to teach philosophy to the youth of Drogheda. Just before the Primate's arrest he nominated Fr Hughes as one of his Vicars General and in a letter to Rome from his prison cell recommended him for a bishopric. It was probably the return of Fr Hughes which allowed the Archbishop to send to Rome for further studies in August 1676 his young cousin Fr Michael Plunkett who had acted as his secretary for three years. In Rome he served for a period as Oliver's agent and was still there at the time of the Archbishop's execution. In 1679 the curate of Armagh, Fr Patrick Donnelly, was sent for further studies to Paris. He was destined one day to become Bishop of Dromore and to go down in history as the Bard of Armagh. These are the best known of the students sent abroad by Oliver; he spared no effort to give the best available training to the most promising of his clergy.

Side by side with the secular clergy the Archbishop had a body of between forty and fifty regular clergy within the archdiocese of Armagh. Some of these, especially the Franciscans, acted as curates in the large rural parishes of Co. Armagh and Co. Tyrone. During Oliver's early years in Ireland there were Franciscan houses in Drogheda (six friars), Dundalk (four friars) and near Armagh (fourteen members); Dominican houses in Drogheda (three friars) and Carlingford (five friars), Augustinians (three friars) and Jesuits (three members) in Drogheda, and a few isolated Cistercians and Carmelites in Co. Louth. The religious houses were dissolved by Government decree of November 1673. There is no clear record of any nun in the archdiocese of Armagh at that time.

The Primate often pays tribute in his letters to the solid virtue and dedication of his priests. There were, however, always a few black sheep who caused him untold worry and pain; to them he was both kind and firm:

1671: I visited my diocese . . . and thanks be to God, of the fifty-six priests who serve in it I found only one of scandalous life. . . . I issued a sentence depriving him of his parish . . . the priest promised me that he would leave the country and go over there to study. The taverns and the women led the miserable fellow astray, and it is a pity, because in other respects he is a capable and intelligent man. 1674: As for my diocese all is quiet apart from two refractory priests.

Oliver looked upon drink as the great source of troubles among the Irish clergy and he found it impossible to recommend any priest who was fond of it for promotion. He had no hesitation in criticising even two of his fellow bishops for what he regarded as over-indulgence and most of the northern Vicars whom he dismissed from office suffered because of this fault. During his first visitation of his suffragan dioceses he noticed the prevalence of drinking and instituted a campaign against it, especially among the clergy, with notable success:

While on visitation in six dioceses in this province I noted that the vice which prevails is the excessive drinking of beer and especially whiskey. . . . I gave a great deal of attention to trying to eradicate this cursed vice, which is mother and nurse to all sorts of scandals and disputes. I ordered under pain of privation of benefices that priests refrain from frequenting taverns and from taking whiskey and indeed the results were very gratifying: these past two months only two priests, and this was on one occasion only, were drunk. And since deeds speak louder than words, I never take a drink between meals. Let us remove this defect from an Irish priest and he will be a saint. . . .

The Primate was kind and patient in dealing with offenders: "I have never deprived anybody unless after four or five warnings, even though the law requires only three." But his firmness in dealing with drunkenness ultimately produced notable results not only in Armagh but throughout the whole of Ulster:

. . . priests who are incorrigible and scandalously drunk will not live in my diocese, even if it should cost me my life. Thanks be to God the deposition and deprivation of Terence O'Kelly, of this McColyn, of Maginn and of two or three others decreed by me in the course of visitation has led to a great reformation of the clergy in the whole province. . . .

## The Tories

Groups of landless men who refused to accept defeat and preyed on the new settlers were a feature of every Irish plantation of the seventeenth century. At no time were they more numerous, however, than during the 1660s, when so many of the Old Irish of the North were bitterly disappointed that the Stuart Restoration brought no restitution of their confiscated lands. In the years immediately before Dr Plunkett's arrival as Archbishop they were strong enough to carry on a guerilla war over a large part of Ulster and Connaught. Some of them, like the redoubtable Redmond O'Hanlon and Patrick Fleming, succeeded in maintaining a code of honour and a patriotic purpose amid their violent activities but others degenerated into common highwaymen and robbers.

The disturbed situation led to considerable harassment of the Catholic population as a whole. Wherever the Tories were strong enough they raided Catholic homes for food and imposed exactions on the Catholic population. The military sent in pursuit of them oppressed the same Catholic families, plundered their homes and killed their livestock. Heavy fines were imposed on the Catholic community who gave the Tories food and shelter; four Catholics were executed in Dungannon for "corresponding with the Tories" and five Co. Tyrone priests were sent to prison because of the disturbed state of that area.

Oliver Plunkett, despite his Anglo-Irish upbringing, had a deep fellow-feeling for the great Ulster families which had lost their lands under Cromwell. His own brother had lost the family estate and mortgages in the Cromwellian confiscations. Hence he could write movingly of the Ulster nobility who had been reduced from princely status to poverty:

It truly moves me to compassion to see high families of the house of O'Neill, O'Donnell, Maguire, Mac Mahon, Maginnis, O'Cahan, O'Kelly, O'Ferrall, who were great princes till the time of Elizabeth and King James, in the memory of my father and many who are yet living; it moves one to compassion, I say, to see their children without property and without maintenance and without means of education; and yet for the faith they suffered joyfully the loss of property.

Condemnations of the Tories were commonplace in the synodal legislation of the Catholic Church in Ireland during the second half of the seventeenth century. Archbishop Plunkett played a prominent part at three of these synods: Dublin (1670), Clones (1670) and Ardpatrick (1678), at each of which the clergy were ordered to warn the faithful not to give any aid to the Tories. But the Archbishop, at the request of the ordinaries of the northern dioceses, also decided to try a direct approach to the Tories on his own.

Having secured the approval of Viceroy Berkeley for direct negotiations with them, he met a large group of Tyrone Tories, mainly O'Neills, Mac Donnells and O'Hagans, on the border of Co. Tyrone in September 1670. Accompanied by only one priest and a servant he spoke to them for an hour about their eternal salvation, the continual danger in which they lived and the sufferings which their fellow-Catholics had to endure because of them. In the name of the Viceroy he offered them pardon for their past deeds on condition that they would go abroad as soldiers to France or Flanders. To encourage them to accept, the pardon was also to cover two of their number in prison under sentence of death and all those Catholics who had been fined on their account.

The Viceroy's original offer seems to have been made to thirty-seven Tories but it is doubtful if so many accepted it. All we can say for certain is that the Archbishop personally accompanied one group of fifteen (of whom six were Mac Donnells) to Dublin and saw them safely aboard ship. He secured £100 from the Viceroy to cover their travelling expenses.

It has been suggested that the Government broke its side of the bargain and in fact transported these Tories to the Barbadoes or North America, but I have come across no evidence for this in contemporary sources. The departure of the Tories brought great peace to Ulster for a few years.

It is surprising that the one voice strongly critical of Oliver's part in the affair was that of the Archbishop of Dublin, not through any sympathy with the Tories but because he claimed Oliver's action was an imprudence which endangered all the Irish clergy. When one recalls that Viceroy Berkeley had little time for Archbishop Talbot, it is hard to avoid the conclusion that what the Archbishop of Dublin really resented was the Viceroy's friendship for the Archbishop of Armagh.

Oliver's negotiations with the Tories were reported to Propaganda by Irishmen resident in Rome and by the letters of Archbishop Talbot. At first the Secretary reacted unfavourably to what had been done — it was a work unbecoming to the episcopal dignity, and could result in a thousand types of calumny, for the bishops would now be held responsible for all crimes — the Primate was therefore to confine himself to exhorting the Catholics to peace, fidelity and other praiseworthy works.

No opposition to the Archbishop's action seems to have come from the Old Irish of the north, the one group who might have been expected to criticise him on patriotic grounds. In fact, the six Vicars of northern dioceses, all of whom were of Old Irish stock, wrote to Rome in October 1670 in warm praise of "a work from which great advantage will be derived by the Catholic body". With this fuller information now available in Rome, the Secretary of Propaganda had second thoughts on the matter and later praised the Primate warmly for what he had achieved.

In view of all this it is strange that the legend has persisted that in acting as mediator between the Tories and the government the Archbishop was in some way acting unpatriotically, and allowed himself to be used as a tool by the government. What was probably responsible for this was the murder of the "Grand Tory", Patrick Fleming, with three of his followers, near Iniskeen, Co. Monaghan, in 1677 as he made his way to go into exile with the Archbishop's safe conduct in his pocket. It is hard to decide if Fleming's death was engineered at high level in order to discredit the Archbishop or was merely the result of an offer of blood-money to a drunken innkeeper. But the poignant lament in Irish composed about Pádraig Pléimionn remained on the lips of the people for over two centuries, and every retelling of his story no doubt reminded the listeners that the Primate's safe conduct had proved of no avail. It was unfortunate for the Primate's memory that the one instance where his policy went astray due to the perfidy of others should have become the instance best remembered in Gaelic tradition. Yet his own letters make clear that at least in 1670 his policy had the approval of the northern Catholics because it restored peace: "This action was applauded by all the Catholics of the province who raised their hands to heaven when they heard it . . . for the past thirty years there has not been such peace in my diocese as it now enjoys."

## Convener of synods

Dr Plunkett was only three months in Ireland when he succeeded in bringing the bishops of the country together for an Episcopal Conference in Dublin. Its chief purpose was to draw up a postulation for the appointment of further bishops and to select a panel of priests suitable for promotion and forward their names to Rome. It was also meant to petition Rome for changes in matrimonial dispensations and for the removal of the Wednesday abstinence, to seek an indulgence for cathedrals and parish churches and to fix the salary of the agent of the Irish bishops in Rome.

The meeting assembled on 17 June 1670 "in Bridge street, in the house of Mr Reynolds" and lasted for three days. It was attended by the four archbishops, and by Bishops Plunkett of Meath and Phelan of Ossory, the only other bishops then in Ireland. It was the first attempt to assemble a National Council of the Irish Church for two decades.

Only three or four days before the conference

began, the Archbishop of Dublin informed Oliver that the Viceroy wished to have a declaration of loyalty from the bishops. Would it provide another split similar to the Remonstrance? Having visited the Viceroy by the secret door in Dublin Castle Oliver satisfied himself that there would be no pressure this time for the inclusion of any clauses derogatory to Papal claims. All six bishops therefore signed a rather harmless formula of loyalty to the king in civil affairs. The Archbishops of Armagh and Dublin clashed as to who should present the address to the Viceroy and again as to who should sign the statutes drawn up by the assembly. These seemed minor differences at the time but out of them, in fact, arose the long drawn out quarrel between the two men, particularly with regard to the Primacy of the Irish Church.

The ten statutes passed by the assembly were not, of course, Oliver Plunkett's own, but several of them, like the decrees of his later synods, bear all the marks of having been inspired by him. Thus there were statutes prohibiting the occupation by one religious order of the house of another and limiting rights of questing. An effort was to be made to eliminate keening at funerals, and corpses were not to be clothed in religious habits. Priests were to warn the people to give no aid to the Tories. No doubt these statutes were all made in the interest of good order and proper decorum, and yet there is in some of them that lack of sympathy with the native thing, an anxiety to have everything in Ireland identical with the Roman way, an attempt to eliminate various local customs rather than to remove their objectionable features, which marks so much Irish ecclesiastical legislation of the seventeenth and eighteenth centuries.

During the summer the new Archbishop made arrangements for the holding of his first Provincial Council, which assembled in Clones in August 1670. It was attended by the ordinaries of all his suffragan dioceses except Clonmacnois (represented by the Vicar-General of Meath) and by the superiors of the Dominican and Franciscan orders. After Mass, Invocation of the Holy Spirit and the *Veni Creator,* the thirteen ecclesiastics got down to the task of drafting legislation for priests and laity.

Only a brief summary of the twenty-eight decrees of the synod can be given here. Priests were forbidden to frequent taverns and market-places, to allow any except females of good reputation into their houses, to bring a lady as pillion on horseback. They were ordered to have a fixed domicile and a fixed place or places for saying Mass. They were not to say Mass twice on Sundays or Holydays except for a grave need, or to take up a collection at the altar more than four times a year. One shilling was fixed as the Mass stipend and two shillings as the dues to be paid by each family per annum. Five shillings was fixed as the annual contribution due from each parish priest to his bishop but one stipend of five shillings was to be paid by every parish priest in the Armagh province to the new Metropolitan. Drinking at wakes, and all-night wakes, were prohibited and no one was to be admitted to wakes except the relations and close friends of the deceased. In the final statute the decrees of the Dublin synod were accepted and promulgated for all the northern dioceses.

Probably the most far-reaching decision of the Synod of Clones, however, was its removal of Terence O'Kelly, Vicar Apostolic of Derry. His unpriestly life had been for many years a source of grave scandal, but everyone who had tried to remove him had been blocked by O'Kelly's citation of him before the civil courts for exercising foreign jurisdiction. Oliver's friendship with the civil authorities prevented this in his case. He persuaded O'Kelly to attend the Synod and to agree to accept its verdict. It deposed him and appointed Eugene Conwell, the Vicar General of Raphoe, in his stead. But when Oliver later went to Derry to institute Conwell, O'Kelly tried to accuse him before the civil court. However, he "found the passes occupied both at the tribunal of the Viceroy and at that of the governor of Ulster, the Earl of Charlemont, and then he cried out at the top of his voice : 'The Italian primate, the Roman primate has unhorsed me !' "

Diocesan synods of his own Armagh clergy were held frequently by Dr Plunkett during the 1670s, roughly every two years. In May 1672 he forbade questing by the religious before the Sunday Masses. No further provincial synod was held by the Primate however until 1678. Then came the Synod of Ard-

patrick, held in the little chapel on the hill overlooking the village of Louth, on 28 August 1678.
Twelve ecclesiastics, including three bishops, attended,
and all the northern dioceses were represented, though
in some cases the Vicar of one diocese acted as proxy
for another.

Again the list of twenty-six decrees is too long
to be given here in full — some of them, in any case,
are much the same as those of the previous synods.
The Tories are condemned once more, priests who
frequent the public market without permission or
who drink whiskey in any public house or public
assembly are liable to a fine of ten shillings, they
are commanded to possess a silver chalice worth
fifty shillings and decent vestments, and to attend
the deanery conferences to be held monthly except
during the three winter months. Other statutes were
clearly directed against those troublesome priests who
had made life difficult for their superiors during the
1670s, including one which prohibited priests from
acting as fosterers of children. As at Clones in 1670
the Synod directed that all priests should pray for
the King, Queen and royal family, for the Viceroy,
and for peace in the country and between Christian
rulers.

Various events of Oliver's life reveal different traits
of his character and personality. The holding of these
synods and the legislation which emanated from them
show how much he was immersed in the Canon Law
atmosphere of the seventeenth century — a reforming

legislator, full of the post-Tridentine passion for attempting to remove abuses by the stroke of a pen.

## Defender of primatial rights

While the contest between Armagh and Dublin regarding the Primacy went back over many centuries, it was the differences between Archbishops Plunkett and Talbot which emerged at the Dublin Synod of 1670 that led to a new round of the primatial dispute being fought out at that particular time. In the Bull of his appointment to Armagh Oliver was styled Primate of Ireland, and in the faculties granted to him Armagh was called "the primatial church of all Ireland". No such titles were used by Rome in the appointment of Archbishop Talbot, but the latter claimed at the Dublin Synod that he had received a commission from King Charles II to "oversee and govern all the Roman Catholic clergy of Ireland". While the initial brush between the two men was in itself a minor disagreement, it no doubt left each determined to defend stoutly what appeared to him to be the right of his own See.

Oliver's understanding of the primatial question was that a primate was in roughly the same position vis-à-vis the archbishops under him as an archbishop was in relation to the bishops under him. The bishop had jurisdiction over a diocese, the archbishop over a province and the primate over a kingdom. Hence the primate could perform a jurisdictional act outside his own province in such cases as an appeal to him, or a matter referred to him by custom, or if the metropolitan See were vacant or the Metropolitan negligent, or the Primate on visitation of another province.

Unfortunately many issues which arose during 1670 and 1671 tended to draw the two men further apart. The Archbishop of Dublin resented Oliver's great influence with the Viceroy and the frequency with which he was called up to Dublin Castle for consultations while he himself remained *persona non grata*. He disagreed with Oliver's handling of the Tory problem: "Here he is with his fifteen bandits in the capital city of my diocese." He was hurt by the fact that Catholic schools were tolerated in Armagh while his own schools in Saggart had been closed. He was displeased that Oliver granted public absolution from censures to the Augustinian Martin French in Dublin.

On the one side Oliver looked on the Archbishop of Dublin as restive and imprudent, too much mixed up in political affairs and not devoting any time to visitation of his diocese. When a meeting of Catholic gentry was held at Oxmanstown at the beginning of February 1671 to take up a collection for Archbishop Talbot's brother, Colonel Richard Talbot, as London agent on behalf of the Irish Catholics, Dr Plunkett attended it in the company of Dr Talbot, but he himself and the Ulster clergy declined to contribute to the fund.

As relations between the two archbishops deterior-
ated, some of the more notable of the laity began
to take sides. Colonel Richard Talbot took his
brother's side, while Oliver's cousin, Sir Nicholas
Plunkett, and Colonel John Fitzpatrick supported
the Armagh side.

It is obvious from the letters sent to Rome by the
two archbishops during the autumn and winter of
1670 that there was no love lost between them at
that time. The internuncio urged them to compose
their differences and Oliver announced happier relations at the time of the Oxmanstown meeting in
February 1671 : "I can assure you that Archbishop
Talbot and I are like blood brothers together, joined
in close union for the public spiritual good and during these eight days of my stay here we were together
every day." This did not prevent him setting out a
summary of the arguments in favour of the primacy
of Armagh which he forwarded to Brussels and Rome,
but relations between the two men remained better
for a large part of 1671.

Then came the Martin French affair and Oliver's
decision in favour of the Dominicans. As he had
foretold the latter was followed by an outburst of
calumnies against him and Oliver soon suspected that
Dr Talbot was not blameless in regard to them.
Certain pasquinades and scurrilous letters defaming
Oliver's character were put into circulation around
Christmas 1671 and he blamed the Archbishop of
Dublin for showing them to some of his associates.

The result was a complete break between the two archbishops for most of 1672.

It seems to have been these scurrilous documents which finally decided Dr Plunkett to go into print in defence of Armagh's primacy. His *Jus Primatiale* was published early in 1672. It is a small octavo volume of forty-six pages in English, subtitled "The Ancient Pre-Eminence of the See of Armagh above all other Archbishops in the kingdom of Ireland, asserted by O.A.T.H.P." (Oliverus Armacanus Totius Hiberniae Primas). The arguments are mainly historical.

On the other side the Archbishop of Dublin now began to cultivate the Franciscans who looked on Oliver Plunkett as their adversary. In addition he accepted an appeal from Patrick McCullen who had been dismissed from his post of Vicar of Clogher by Oliver early in 1672. He did the same with an Armagh priest Edmond Maginn who had been suspended by the Primate in the summer of 1672. By virtue of a new commission for the superintendence of the Catholic clergy which Dr Talbot claimed to have received from King Charles II, he ordered Dr Plunkett not to ordain so many priests, to withdraw his decree that the branch of the O'Reillys nicknamed Clann an Chaoich should resume the surname O'Reilly, and to receive no further appeals from Dublin.

Rome was very alarmed by the pitch which the controversy had reached in 1671 and 1672 and ordered both sides to keep silent and to send the arguments in favour of their Sees in writing to Rome. It seems likely that this order had not reached Dr Plunkett before the publication of his book, but, together with the advice of some of the other bishops, it prevented the Archbishop of Dublin from going into print at once with his reply. "Since my arrival here, I have not omitted to exhort them both to peace," wrote Bishop John Brenan of Waterford, ". . . they are, both one and the other, touchy and of a hot disposition . . . and in my opinion they would be displeased to receive an admonition from an inferior bishop."

It was the arrival in Ireland towards the end of 1672 of the new Bishop of Killaloe, John O'Molony, that finally effected a reconciliation. Having first made peace between Colonel Talbot and Colonel Fitzpatrick he then brought the two archbishops together on 19 November 1672 and they became good friends. "The Archbishop of Dublin and myself are like two real brothers, we agree so well," wrote Oliver early in 1673, "so also are Colonel Fitzpatrick and Colonel Talbot."

But while the controversy never again reached the bitterness of 1672 it was not completely buried by Dr O'Molony's intervention. After Essex became Viceroy, certain Dominicans accused Archbishop Talbot of the exercise of "foreign jurisdiction" and the levying of money, and a commission was set up to investigate the charges. Among the witnesses called to give

evidence was Dr Plunkett and on 8 May 1673 he
gave a full account of the Dublin Synod of 1670 and
the Oxmanstown meeting of 1671. When the order
for the expulsion of all bishops was later issued,
mentioning Peter Talbot by name, the Archbishop of
Dublin was inclined to blame his colleague in Armagh
for his banishment. Just before his departure he had
pronounced a marriage valid, but the parties, on
appeal, received a decree of nullity from Armagh.
The Archbishop of Armagh, however, later apologised
for this decision which was based on incomplete
information.

In exile Dr Talbot published his reply to Oliver's
book under the title *Primatus Dublinensis*. It is a
book of eighty-five pages in Latin, published at Lille
in 1674.

The outburst of persecution and the exile of Archbishop Talbot hushed the primatial controversy during
the next few years. However, there is some evidence
that in 1678 Dr Plunkett was preparing for the press
a reply to the Lille publication but the new banishment order of 1678 followed by the arrest of the two
archbishops put a final closure on the controversy
during Oliver's lifetime.

In Dublin Castle Dr Plunkett found himself in a
cell adjacent to that occupied by the Archbishop of
Dublin. The latter addressed him an apology, asking
pardon for any fault which, in the heat of the dispute,
he might have committed. When Dr Talbot, seriously
ill in mind and body, seemed in grave danger of death

at the beginning of June 1680, Oliver burst through his guards and rushed to his cell to console and absolve the dying archbishop. It was the final reconciliation between two men who had battled strenuously for the rights of their respective Sees during life but were linked in a last embrace by a persecution of which both were victims.

## Protestant friends

Not long after Oliver's arrival in Ireland Archbishop Margetson of Armagh (1663-78) expressed a wish to meet him and Oliver visited the Protestant Primate:

> The Protestant primate asked to speak to me and I visited him, and he gave me precedence in his own house, as well as those titles which belong to me. We had a meeting of an hour's duration and he promised me that he would never interfere with me in the smallest matter; indeed he has given me permission to have schools with Catholic masters in my diocese. . . .
>
> In fine, all, both Catholics and non-Catholics, have great respect for me because they know I enjoy the favour of the Viceroy and because His Excellency has been pleased on several occasions to speak of me in the presence of others with great esteem.

Archbishop Margetson was English born and had suffered much during the English Civil War. Through him Oliver became acquainted with Dr Dudley Loftus, the celebrated Orientalist. He found Loftus very friendly and they became close friends.

During the remainder of 1670 Oliver visited him
on at least four occasions. As Loftus was Vicar
General of the Church of Ireland Primate of Armagh,
Oliver's friendship with him proved a source of protection for the Jesuits and their schools. Oliver also
hoped that through the good offices of Loftus he
would be granted permission to consult the medieval
Registers of Armagh. It is obvious from several references in Oliver's book on the primacy of Armagh
(1672) that he had access to the Registers while
compiling it.

In several letters to Rome Oliver praised the learning and friendliness of Dr Loftus. In fact the Archbishop felt that Loftus was really very Catholic in
outlook and that only the position which he held in
the Church of Ireland prevented him from giving his
allegiance to Rome :

The Protestant primate is very favourably disposed
to the Catholics and his Vicar General, Doctor
Dudley Loftus, the most learned man the Protestants have, is our best friend. He is very well
versed in all the oriental languages and in canon
law and in Catholic casuistry. In my opinion, if he
were not afraid of losing his income he would
become a Catholic — he already is one in his
beliefs. He is writing to Cardinal Barberini; please
get His Eminence to write him a kindly reply.

Another Irish Protestant who proved a staunch
friend of Archbishop Plunkett during his first year in

Ireland was William Caulfeild, 1st Viscount Charlemont (d. 1671). His son was married to Archbishop Margetson's daughter. As Charlemont was President of Ulster his support proved very useful to the Archbishop on more than one occasion :

> The Earl of Charlemont, president of this province, is so well disposed towards me that he defends me from every annoyance. Once when I was in the town of Dungannon to give confirmation and being impeded by the governor of that place, the Earl of Charlemont delivered a vigorous rebuke to the governor. He told me to come to his palace and give confirmation there and say Mass also if I wished.
>
> The magistrate of the city of Armagh gave orders that all the Catholics of that town accompany him to the Protestant church every Sunday under pain of being fined half a *scudo* per person every time they missed. I had recourse to the president against this decree; he ordered its revocation and gave instructions that neither priests nor other Catholics were to be molested.

These incidents took place during 1670; early in the following year Oliver was reporting further generosity towards himself on the part of Charlemont shortly before the latter's death in May 1671 :

> This Earl of Charlemont has not molested a single cleric since my arrival; he is very friendly towards me; indeed on one occasion he said to me, seeing that I was somewhat afraid : "Don't be afraid, no

man will lay a finger on you; and when you want to give confirmation, don't go to the mountains, come here to the courtyard of my palace." He gave me a garden and a fine orchard with two fields, and a fine house for my lifetime — it is in a lovely situation.

Henry Moore, 1st Earl of Drogheda (d. 1675), also proved a good friend of the Primate and of his flock. As he had no Protestants living on his estate, he allowed the churches (with bells) to be used by the priests for Catholic worship. The Countess of Drogheda (an English lady, aunt of the Earl of Sunderland) invited the Archbishop to dinner and treated him with great courtesy.

It was not long before letters began to arrive in Rome complaining of Oliver's too close intimacy with Protestants. The first complainant apparently confused Dublin and Armagh and this gave Oliver the chance to issue a humorous denial, asserting that: "As regards the Protestant Archbishop of Dublin and his vicar, God is my witness and I speak no lie, since the day I was born I have not spoken to them and I do not know the colour of their beard." Later Oliver wrote that the complaints were due to petty jealousy and that his friendship with leading Protestants was beneficial to the Church. Yet the complaints were renewed periodically during his whole decade of work in Ireland. In 1677 similar complaints made to Rome against the Archbishop were referred to Archbishop Brenan of Cashel, and the latter repudiated the suggestion that Archbishop Plunkett was too familiar with Protestant ministers.

During the summer of 1679 Fr Anthony Daly, O.F.M., former guardian of the Franciscans of Armagh, drew up in Louvain a list of eight complaints against the Archbishop including the perennial *nimia familiaritas cum hetherodoxis.* A copy of these complaints was submitted to the Internuncio in Brussels by Fr Patrick Maginn, former chaplain to Queen Catherine, and another copy was forwarded to Rome by Daly himself for submission to the Pope and Cardinals. Rome brought the complaints to Oliver's attention and it is a sad commentary on the dissensions of those years that Oliver's first letter after his imprisonment in Dublin Castle had to be a letter of self-defence against these accusations made by his fellow priests.

The respect which the ordinary Protestants of his diocese had for Archbishop Plunkett was made clear on the occasion of his trial in Dundalk in July 1680. Although all Catholics had been excluded from the jury, the Archbishop "did not object, knowing well that all the Protestants of my district regarded Mac Moyer as an associate of the Tories. . . . I also was aware that they all believed that what Mac Moyer swore against me was a mere fable". The Church of Ireland Bishop of Meath, Dr Henry Jones, was strongly anti-Catholic and made strenuous efforts to have Oliver's trial transferred from Dundalk and to obtain witnesses against him. It should be a source of satisfaction to Irish Protestants that apart from Dr Jones no one else from their ranks was an accomplice in his death.

## Relations with the Franciscans

Even before his return to Ireland as Archbishop, Oliver Plunkett's relations with some of the Irish Franciscans were a little strained. During his years as professor in Rome he became closely acquainted with the Franciscan community in St Isidore's and recommended one of them, Fr Francis Molloy, author of *Lucerna Fidelium* and of the first printed grammar of Irish for the bishopric of Clonmacnois.

We do not know if his request for the return of the "Armagh Cross" at the time of his departure from Rome was acceded to. Some of the Ulster Franciscans expected one of their own number, Dr Patrick Duffy (afterwards Bishop of Clogher), to be appointed Archbishop of Armagh.

On his return journey through Belgium Oliver visited the Irish Franciscan College of Louvain where he met a large community of fifty friars, fifteen of whom had only recently arrived from Ireland. Correspondence from the Bishop of Ardagh had complained about the importunity of the friars in Ireland who quested for alms before they allowed the parish priests to say Mass on Sundays. From Brussels Dr Plunkett addressed a letter to Rome a fortnight before his consecration urging that the number of friars in Ireland should be strictly limited, that the number of novitiates should be reduced and novices should be trained in one of the Continental houses and that no friar should be allowed to return to Ireland from a Continental country without the permission of the local Papal Nuncio.

A week later he returned to the subject in a further letter, complaining of the inadequacy of the training given in the Irish novitiates, the wide powers to dispense in matrimonial cases claimed by the Irish Franciscans and the rivalry between themselves and the Dominicans. The latter is the Archbishop's first reference to a problem which was to prove one of his greatest headaches over the next decade.

Despite these letters the new Primate's reception by the Irish Franciscan Province seems to have been cordial enough at first. A bust of the Primate was set up in the Library of St Isidore's in Rome. Apart from the few friars who still adhered to Coppinger, the anti-Provincial elected during the split of 1666, Oliver was able to report from Ireland that "the Franciscan fathers who adhere to the new provincial show me great affection". On his first visitation of his archdiocese, during the early summer of 1670, the Archbishop made contact with all the religious communities and was particularly impressed by the Franciscans of Armagh:

Near Armagh there is a convent of Franciscan friars in which there are twelve friars, good religious who keep a large public chapel and a novitiate. The

Protestants themselves send them alms. They sing Mass formally and within the convent they wear the habit.

Shortly afterwards the Franciscan Provincial expressed to the Archbishop his need for power to expel incorrigible friars after a threefold warning and Dr Plunkett sought this power for him from Rome.

It was the Archbishop's visitation of various northern dioceses during the summer and autumn of 1670 that brought home to him the serious scandals which the Franciscan-Dominican conflict was causing. Rivalry between the two orders had begun to appear in the 1640s when their increasing membership as a result of greater toleration and the impact of their new Continental houses had led to differences regarding their respective rights of questing. These differences had to be suppressed during the Cromwellian era but they broke out on a more serious scale in the middle 1660s. Within the Armagh province the former Dominican houses at Carlingford, Newtownards and Gaula (Co. Fermanagh), from which the Dominicans had retired during the persecution, were at issue. The peace of four dioceses — Armagh, Down and Connor, Dromore and Clogher — was being seriously disturbed. In some areas it was the right of questing which was disputed, but in the case of Gaula the actual building had been seized by both sides. Each order preached against the other and on occasions they came to blows. The secular clergy and the laity also became involved in the quarrel and in several parishes long lists were compiled of parishioners who asserted that they had never seen Dominicans there.

Both sides could back up their claims by an appeal to the past. Historically there was no doubt that the three friaries had belonged to the Dominicans in pre-Reformation times but the Order had not occupied them for nearly a century until the 1660s. The Franciscans could claim to have been active in the same areas for most of the intervening period. Against this the Dominicans countered that prescription did not take effect at a time of persecution. Judged on the documents which have so far come to light the majority of the secular clergy and laity supported the Franciscans in the dispute. The vicars of the various northern dioceses also supported them.

The Synod of Clones took no action about the dispute as the two orders promised to come to an amicable settlement among themselves. They failed to do so and instead each instructed a representative to present its case before Propaganda. At home the dispute continued to give rise to scandalous scenes during the winter of 1670-71.

In various letters to Rome Dr Plunkett expressed his willingness to decide the issue if given authority by the Holy See. Yet he was conscious that a decision in favour of either order would give rise to a storm of abuse from the other:

If I decide in favour of the Dominicans, lo and behold all the Franciscans will write and speak a thousand calumnies, that this primate is the enemy of the Franciscans etc. and *vice versa* if I decide in favour of the Franciscans. Notwithstanding this, if Your Lordship or the Internuncio writes to me and tells me that I may decide these disputes of theirs and that I should decide them, I shall decide them fearlessly and I know that my decision will have effect.

At the end of May or beginning of June 1671 the Archbishop received authority from Rome to decide the issue. He planned to visit each of the controverted districts: "I will receive their allegations and proofs and afterwards pronounce judgment in accordance with these proofs and documents." One final meeting near Dundalk of more than twenty from each side had failed to bring peace — it began as a friendly discussion but almost came to blows — and there was nothing for it now except a primatial decision.

Archbishop Plunkett visited the dioceses of Down, Dromore and Clogher in July 1671 and collected evidence from both sides. He became ill during his visit to Clogher. Before the end of the month he indicated to Rome that his decision would favour the Dominicans, no matter what reaction it might provoke.

Having first consulted the Bishop of Meath and the Vicars of Meath and Kilmore and associated them with his decision, the Archbishop issued his decree from Dundalk on 11 October 1671, declaring that the Dominicans were free to quest for alms in the dioceses of Armagh, Clogher, Down and Dromore and ordering all priests to accept this under pain of *ipso facto* suspension. In view of the widespread public support for the Franciscans it was a courageous decision, though one wonders if some more subtle form of compromise rather than a decision which placed one side completely in the right and the other side completely in the wrong might not have been more prudent in the circumstances.

The violent reaction which Oliver anticipated was not long delayed. "It seemed as though hell itself was let loose against me," he wrote later. Many calumnies against the Primate were circulated. Fights between religious occurred at the altar both in Co. Louth and Co. Tyrone. The Franciscans decided to appeal and despatched Fr Paul O'Neill to Rome as their representative. In the library of St Isidore's the Archbishop's bust was decapitated by two rebellious novices. At home Fr Bonaventure O'Quinn, guardian of Armagh Friary, was appointed procurator of the Ulster Franciscans and on 19 March 1672 he appealed to the Pope against the Archbishop's decision.

The Congregation of Propaganda gave no decision for several years. In Ireland the outbreak of persecution in 1673 closed down the houses of both orders and put an end for the time being to their dissensions. Finally, in 1678, the Sacred Congregation pronounced in favour of the Dominicans and thus confirmed Oliver Plunkett's decision.

It would be wrong to assume that Oliver's decision in favour of the Dominicans was the only or even the main cause of the friction between himself and the Franciscans. Much more basic was the question of where the jurisdiction of an exempt religious order ended and that of the Archbishop began. Because of the persecutions many Irish Franciscans had been granted very wide powers by Rome. Oliver, on the other hand, was a staunch believer in having all ecclesiastical power centralised in the hierarchy. To a man who for many years had seen everything carried out canonically in Rome, the spectacle of farmhouse novitiates, of friars who in times of persecution had to don lay attire, and of a clerical body in some areas as numerous as the secular clergy, who for all practical purposes were subject only to their own superiors, convinced him of the need for sweeping reforms. Many of his letters to Rome, therefore, are strongly critical of the Franciscans. He even advocated a division of the Irish Franciscans into two provinces, each with its own provincial.

There can be no doubt that in all this Oliver's motives were pure and that he acted always in what he considered the best interests of the Church. Yet it was only natural that the Franciscans should look on it as interference in the affairs of an exempt Order by an outsider and resent it accordingly. His motives were therefore suspect and his actions often misinterpreted. The guardian of Dundalk reminded him of the treatment which his predecessor Richard Fitzralph had met at the hands of the religious orders and threatened him with the same fate. The guardian of Armagh, according to what Oliver heard, instigated the Tories to kill him. A number of friars, spearheaded by Fr Anthony Daly, instituted a process against him in Rome. Two dissolute Franciscans, who had been expelled from the Order because of their evil lives, gave evidence against him in London.

Yet from the scaffold at Tyburn Oliver pleaded that the action of the two unfortunates should not be held against the Franciscan Order as a whole :

> This wicked act, being a defect of persons, ought not to reflect upon the Order of St Francis or upon the Roman Catholic clergy, it being well known that there was a Judas among the twelve Apostles. . . .

It was the epilogue of a saint to what was probably the saddest chapter of his life story.

# 3 Trial and execution

## Arrest and imprisonment

Despite the hunt for all bishops, Oliver continued his ministrations throughout Ulster until the middle of October 1679, when he learned that the Bishop of Meath was dangerously ill. He refused to allow the danger of arrest to keep him away from the death-bed of his old teacher and friend. Having cut off his hair and beard, and put on a light-coloured wig, he set out for the capital under the assumed name of Mr Meleady.

But unknown to Oliver a very secret instruction had been issued to Ormonde by the British Privy Council on 21 October 1679 to arrest himself and Bishop Tyrrell of Clogher. The background to this instruction had been a letter handed in to the Duke of York (the future King James II) in Brussels accusing Colonel John Fitzpatrick of plotting, with the aid of the two bishops, to bring a French army to Ireland.

Ormonde entrusted the task of tracking down the Primate to Sir Hans Hamilton of Hamiltonsbawn near Armagh. When Hamilton made known to a local parish priest that he wished to communicate urgently with the Primate, the priest innocently revealed that he was staying near The Naul and gave details of his disguise. The Bishop of Meath had passed away on 18 November, leaving to Oliver his altar utensils, books and *pontificalia* for his lifetime. But less than three weeks later Oliver was arrested in Dublin on 6 December. He was immediately placed in close confinement in a cell in Dublin Castle.

For six weeks the prisoner was kept in solitary confinement. Even his servant was refused access to him during this period. His papers were examined and found to be innocuous. He was not personally examined either by Ormonde or by the committee set up to interrogate suspects.

On 16 January 1680 his servant and some friends were allowed to visit him and he was permitted to write letters. It is a tragic commentary on the dissensions among the Ulster clergy that his first letter to Rome, written on the following day, was mainly taken up with defending himself against the accusations of an Armagh priest. It was a foretaste of the unscrupulous part which would be played by a number of the clergy in his forthcoming trial.

## The plot

Oliver Plunkett was in Dublin Castle for three months before anyone came forward with an offer to provide evidence against him. This in itself should have made the authorities doubly suspicious of the "informations" lodged against him later. During those three months Ormonde was the only man in Ireland who knew that there was more behind his arrest than the Archbishop's failure to obey the order banishing him from Ireland.

But it was well known in Ireland that some of the Whig opponents of King Charles II in London were on the lookout for anyone who could back up the assertions of Titus Oates by providing evidence of a similar conspiracy in Ireland. A few prisoners in Munster jails had come forward during 1679 but their stories proved of little value. Then, with the arrest of Oliver Plunkett, the spotlight turned from Munster to the Archbishop's own diocese, where a number of jailbirds got the idea of securing pardon for themselves and obtaining financial rewards by providing evidence which would link him with the Popish Plot.

The plan was probably first thought of by a prisoner in Dundalk Jail, William Hetherington, who "sold" it to his fellow-prisoner, Edmund Murphy. Hetherington, a Protestant from Ganderstown, Co. Louth, had served as a Tory-hunter in the past, but was imprisoned in Dundalk for correspondence with the Tories and later in the Dublin Marshalsea for non-payment of debt. Murphy, former parish priest of Killeavy, Co. Armagh, had been suspended by the Archbishop for drunkenness and associating with Tories and was imprisoned in Dundalk for the latter. In the jail there Hetherington convinced him that there was a bright future for anyone who could provide evidence of an Irish dimension to the Popish Plot.

## Priest witnesses

Hetherington and Murphy both escaped from prison and the former crossed to London where he was taken under his wing by Lord Shaftesbury. Having been examined before the Council he was sent back to Ireland under the care of two pursuivants to collect Murphy and other witnesses who could throw light on a Popish Plot in Ireland. Along with Murphy and three soldiers the party made its way to the north of Ireland and arrested three further priests, who would, it was hoped, corroborate and amplify the testimony of Murphy. They were two parish priests of South Armagh, Callaghan and Feenan, and Friar John Moyer.

Moyer, at one time Vicar of the Armagh Franciscan community, but later suspended by the Primate, had been carrying on a personal vendetta against the Archbishop for several years. He had refused to accept the 1671 decision in favour of the Dominicans, was notorious for drunkenness, and had been convicted at Armagh Assizes of giving powder and shot to the Tories. As early as December 1676 he had given evidence before Sir Hans Hamilton that the Primate was conspiring to bring in a French army and he had repeated his accusations in subsequent years. Neither Essex nor Ormonde had hitherto attached any importance to the fellow's ravings, but in the new situation in which Ormonde himself was now being linked with the Popish Plot, he could no longer afford to ignore them.

The four priests were examined orally before the
Privy Council in London in May 1680 but their
limited knowledge of English made interrogation
difficult and they were therefore ordered to submit
their informations in writing on the following day.
It is hardly likely that men whose knowledge of
spoken English was so poor were able to prepare
written submissions without the assistance of others.
Moyer repeated once more his allegations about the
Primate's treasonable correspondence; the others were
concerned only with the Primate's exercise of jurisdiction. It was decided to send the witnesses and their
depositions back to Ireland so that Oliver Plunkett
might now be prosecuted on the basis of them.
Hetherington, who had no material evidence to offer,
remained on in London.

## Preparations for the trial

Back in Ireland Murphy was only too conscious of
the fact that he was now liable to be re-arrested on
the capital charge of corresponding with the Tories.
Various efforts were made to obtain pardon for him
during June without avail. The hostile treatment
which the four witnesses had received on their return
to Dublin made Moyer fearful about giving evidence
against the Primate in Dundalk. Accordingly, he
petitioned Ormonde and called personally on the
Lord Chief Justice in an effort to have the trial
transferred to Dublin. When this failed, representations were made in London to the same purpose,

and the English Privy Council finally ordered on 21 July that the trial of Oliver Plunkett should take place before the King's Bench in Dublin. But the order had come too late. On the very same morning the judges had left Dublin for Dundalk for the opening of the sessions on the following day. The prisoner was also on his way thither.

## Trial at Dundalk

Oliver Plunkett was put on trial at Dundalk on 23 July 1680. The judges were Baron Hartstonge and Judge Cusack. John Lyndon was prosecuting counsel; the prisoner was not allowed any defence counsel in court. An order had been issued that no Catholic should be allowed on the jury, but the Primate made no objection, so confident was he that he would receive justice from the Protestants of Co. Louth.

The proceedings opened with the submission to the jury of two bills of indictment, one for treason and one for exercising papal jurisdiction. Moyer's depositions provided most of the evidence but Callaghan's seem to have been used also to support the charge of exercising papal jurisdiction. Although legal procedure at that time did not permit the accused to be informed of the charges until the day of the trial, the Archbishop had got knowledge of them beforehand. On being asked by one of the judges how he knew, he replied that some of those who had heard Moyer make the charges at Mass had informed him.

The Archbishop's petition to the Irish Privy Council for an order for the appearance of witnesses had been refused and three of his letters from Dublin Castle asking witnesses to appear on his behalf had been intercepted. Nevertheless, thirty-two witnesses turned up to testify on his behalf — priests (including friars) and laymen, Protestants and Catholics.

The trial broke down on the second day through the absence of the prosecuting witnesses. Murphy had disappeared suddenly and was already in London before the trial began. Moyer may have appeared on the first day but refused to attend on 24 July, alleging that he awaited the return of Murphy. After being detained for four days in the old jail of Dundalk (situated at the corner of Church Street and York Street) Oliver Plunkett was sent back to Dublin Castle.

## Transfer to London

"The manner of proceeding here in criminal cases seems very strange to me," wrote Oliver on his return to his cell in Dublin. An accused person was kept in ignorance of the charge until the day of his trial. He was allowed no counsel for the defence and his witnesses were not sworn. He had to be acquitted at three separate trials before regaining his freedom. As the next assizes were not due in Dundalk until the end of March 1681, Oliver was advised to apply for a transfer of the trial to Dublin where it could take place in November 1680. He hoped that the Dundalk jury would be recalled for the Dublin hearing.

But just as his enemies had striven behind the scenes to get the first trial removed from Dundalk and failing that had ensured its collapse there, they now worked might and main in London to have the trial removed from Ireland altogether. To his credit it must be said that Ormonde vigorously resisted this move, claiming that it was unlawful and without precedent to try a man in England for an offence allegedly committed in Ireland. But the Whig leaders were not going to be dissuaded now by possible illegalities. On 6 October Ormonde was ordered to send Oliver Plunkett for trial in London.

The Primate's last weeks in Dublin Castle brought him to the verge of destitution. The Dundalk "trial" had been costly; he had borne the expenses of travel and maintenance for his thirty-two witnesses, all for nothing. He had distributed ten pounds among the guards and servants of the sheriff. To cover the heavy costs he had to sell some of his few personal items of property and even to pawn his chalice and pectoral cross. At a time when everything seemed to be going against him he learned that two further disreputable friars, George Coddan and Paul Gormley, had purchased their release from prison by offering to give evidence against him.

On the night of 24 October 1680 Oliver Plunkett sailed from Ireland for the last time. On board ship he wrote an urgent letter to the Internuncio in Brussels beseeching him to get money sent on for him to a London Catholic merchant. The Archbishop was placed in the charge of four of the Royal Guards under the command of a certain George Wakefield who delivered him safely at Newgate prison on 29 October and was paid £40 from secret service money in the following January for his trouble. James McKenna accompanied him to London, faithful to the last.

In Newgate the Archbishop was placed in solitary confinement. It was bad enough to be confined in irons in this gruesome dungeon but to add insult to injury the prisoner had to pay for his room and food, even for the shackles on his legs. In a few weeks his money ran out and he petitioned "to be maintained upon his Majesty's charge". The granting of this petition allowed the keeper ten shillings weekly for the prisoner's support. But when McKenna brought a change of linen to the prison, he was promptly arrested and lodged in a nearby cell. The Archbishop's petition to be allowed his services was refused.

On 4 November Oliver was examined before a sub-committee of the Privy Council. He made a good impression, much better than Edmund Murphy, who was brought along to make his accusations in his presence. No other witnesses against him seem to have been available and the Archbishop was brought back to his cell of solitude. But later in the month Moyer, Callaghan and Feenan arrived back in London from Ireland, the vanguard of that "battalion of testimony" who would bring the Primate to the scaffold.

## Search for witnesses

Meanwhile the north of Ireland was being scoured for further possible witnesses. On 26 October 1680, when Oliver was en route for London, the English House of Lords had empowered three messengers to go to Ireland to collect witnesses. This was followed shortly by the decision of the English Privy Council to grant pardon for their own offences, and payment out of treasury funds to all who would give evidence within two months. If pardons and payments were not sufficient the messengers were empowered to have potential witnesses arrested and brought over by force.

Among the priests for whose arrest warrants were issued were Brian MacGurk, Dean of Armagh, and Henry Hughes, its Vicar General, Manus O'Quinn, parish priest of Creggan and Brian Hullen or Holland, parish priest of Muckno. MacGurk and Hughes escaped the net but the other two priests were arrested. About a dozen northerners in all were rounded up and were brought to London in mid-January 1681 by the messenger who had visited Ulster, Owen Murphy. When these twelve are added to the original four witnesses of 1680 and account is taken of Gormley and McCoddan who had arrived before them, and of Florence Weyer and Hugh Hanlon who followed them, it will be seen that at least twenty Ulstermen were brought to London in the effort to condemn their Archbishop. They were divided evenly between priests and laymen; they included four secular priests of Armagh, two secular priests of Clogher and four Franciscans. Not all these priests of course appeared in court against the Archbishop. Among those who did not it is necessary to single out the heroic figure of Brian Holland, parish priest of Muckno, who was permitted to return to Ireland in the spring as his evidence was of no use against the Primate, but courageously headed for London again during the summer in the hope of giving evidence on his behalf.

## In dungeon dark

Only on very rare occasions do we get a glimpse of Oliver Plunkett's thoughts and activities during the six long months that he languished in solitary confinement amid the dirt, noise, cold and drunkenness of Newgate. One such occasion occurred at the very beginning of the period, on 10 November 1680, when he appeared before the bar of the House of Lords and denied that he had any correspondence with France. On being asked if he knew about any conspiracies he expressed doubt that there was any conspiracy against the English but declared that on about a hundred occasions his own life had been threatened if he prosecuted the Tories.

The curtain lifts again on 12 February 1681 when the bill of indictment against the Primate was presented to the Grand Jury of Westminster. But the witnesses contradicted each other so blatantly that the Grand Jury rejected the bill. This was equivalent to saying that the Grand Jury did not believe in the prisoner's guilt. It was necessary therefore to school the witnesses better before the next attempt.

The rejection of the bill by the Grand Jury encouraged James McKenna to present a petition to the Privy Council on 25 February seeking permission to speak to the Archbishop. McKenna had now been nearly four months in Newgate without any charge having been brought against him and without once meeting his master. He feared that Oliver's old complaint of gallstones was being aggravated by the solitary confinement. The Attorney-General was instructed to investigate McKenna's case and report back. On 9 March he reported that McKenna's imprisonment had been due solely to the fact that he was a papist and as such not allowed in London, and the Privy Council therefore ordered his release on substantial bail.

## Sent for trial

It was only in the following month that the Westminster Grand Jury finally found a true bill against the Archbishop and returned him for trial before the King's Bench on a charge of high treason. By that time a petition had been presented to the King requesting that the Archbishop's solitary confinement should be mitigated for reasons of health. On 22 April the King and Privy Council decided that he might be given as much liberty within the prison as the governor would deem consistent with security and might receive visitors but only in the hearing of the governor or his representative. A further petition from the Archbishop on 27 April brought the restoration of his papers after they had been examined by the Attorney-General.

On 3 May 1681 Oliver Plunkett was arraigned for high treason before the King's Bench. It was the opening day of the Trinity Term and the procession of the judges in state through the city brought a larger crowd than usual to Westminster Hall. The prisoner objected to being tried in England for an offence allegedly committed in Ireland but was overruled by Lord Chief Justice Pemberton. He pleaded *Not Guilty* and asked for time to have his witnesses brought from Ireland. The trial was fixed for Wednesday 8 June, five weeks away, and he was given permission to see his servant in the presence of the governor. His request that a priest be permitted access to him was however turned down.

Fr Emmanuel Curtis, a recent biographer of Oliver Plunkett, called attention to a serious error in the indictment against the prisoner. The date of the Archbishop's alleged treason, as given in the indictment, is 1 December in the 32nd year of Charles II. This can only be 1 December 1680, at which date the Archbishop was a close prisoner in Dublin castle.

## A race against time

Five weeks was an extremely short period in which to assemble witnesses from Ireland but the attempt must be made. The Archbishop decided to call eight witnesses only. They would cost £20 each. With John Plunkett, a relative of the Archbishop, as his companion McKenna set out to gather them in Ireland. After two days at sea their boat was blown back to London. They then took coach for Holyhead only to find that a strong west wind made the journey impossible and further precious time was wasted. It was 19 May before they landed in Dublin. Less than three weeks remained.

Plunkett set out for the nearby territory of Louth and Meath but McKenna had to go as far as Armagh and Derry. In the circumstances it was a magnificent achievement to collect the full complement of eight witnesses. But on arrival in Dublin the witnesses refused to cross to England until the King would grant them safe conduct. It did not come through until 6 June. The key witness was a certain Edmund Fay of Co. Meath, who had been a fellow-prisoner with Hetherington and Murphy in Dundalk Jail in the previous year. He was prepared to testify that they had invented the charges against the Archbishop there, and that Hetherington had offered him money to join them in giving evidence.

Knowing the hostility and dangers that awaited the Archbishop's witnesses in London, one can understand their reluctance to put their freedom — even their lives — at risk. It is harder to excuse the refusal of the Irish court officials to supply the Archbishop's messengers with copies of the criminal record of

Murphy, Moyer and the other Crown witnesses without an express order from the English courts.

By June 6 McKenna and Plunkett were back in London empty-handed. On that day the Archbishop appealed to the Court of King's Bench for twelve extra days to allow his witnesses to arrive. His petition was turned down. On the following day, as a last resort, he addressed a petition directly to the King pleading for the extra twelve days and backing up his petition with an affidavit sworn by John Plunkett indicating what important evidence the witnesses would be able to provide. The documents were ignored.

## Judges and jury

On Wednesday 8 June 1681 Oliver Plunkett stood alone before his enemies in Westminster Hall. He could expect little sympathy from judges, jury, accusers or audience. All authorities are agreed that in the Popish Plot trials English legal practice reached its lowest level. The trial of Oliver Plunkett was one of the most blatantly unjust of the lot.

It was presided over by the new Lord Chief Justice, Sir Francis Pemberton, a suave and scholarly bigot in his early forties. By his side sat Justice Dolben, a zealous Protestant, and Justice Jones, a hot-tempered Welshman. Counsel for the prosecution included the Attorney-General Sir Robert Sawyer, the Solicitor-General Heneage Finch, Serjeant Jeffreys who would one day become notorious as the Hanging Judge and Mr Heath who led for the Crown.

In regard to the jury it is sufficient to indicate that two of them, including their foreman, Sir John Roberts, had been members of the jury which had sent five Jesuits to their death at Tyburn three years earlier. The Archbishop raised this matter before they were sworn, only to have his query brushed aside contemptuously by the Chief Justice. Yet he can hardly have been reassured as he listened to the names which were called out: Harriott . . . Ashurst . . . Bucknall . . . Gowre . . . Pagett . . . Easby.

## The trial begins

The Archbishop was summoned to keep his right hand raised above his head while the long indictment in legal jargon was read out. Heath led for the prosecution, giving a summary of the indictment in plain language. He was followed by Maynard who accused the Archbishop of having been appointed to his high office to promote the Popish Plot and of using his position to raise men and money for this purpose. Then came Sawyer who painted a vivid picture of the Primate recruiting men, collecting money and examining the ports suitable for a French landing before finally selecting Carlingford.

The Crown wished to prove the existence of a plot for a French invasion of Ireland before attempting to saddle it on the Archbishop. Of the nine witnesses called for the prosecution at the Archbishop's trial, the first four were obviously meant to provide evidence of a general nature.

## Lay witnesses

The first witness called was Florence Weyer, tragic descendant of the family of Mac an Mhaoir which for centuries had served as keepers of the Book of Armagh. Deprived by the Ulster Plantation of the eight townlands of Ballymoyer, they had been reduced to the status of small farmers, and the last keeper, a school-master by profession, had pledged the Book of Armagh for £5 to enable him to travel to London.

Florence traced the plot to bring in the French back to the activities of the Tories in the 1660s; in this context it was easy for him to explain the Archbishop's efforts to send the Tories to France as a further step in a Franco-Irish military alliance. He claimed to have seen the Primate's orders for the collection of money and mentioned Carlingford as the port chosen for the French landing. But under the Primate's questioning he admitted that he had never seen him there and that he (Weyer) had done nothing for years with his supposed information about the invasion project.

The next three witnesses made a poor impression on their hearers. Both Henry O'Neill and his son Phelim referred to meetings held in 1678 and Owen Murphy admitted that he knew nothing except what he learned from his namesake Edmund.

## Priest witnesses

The priest witnesses all appeared during the second half of the trial and were meant to pin the main responsibility for the plot on the shoulders of the Archbishop. Hugh Duffy, the former friar who had served for a while as curate to Edmund Murphy in Killeavy, claimed to have had access to private information in his capacity as chaplain to Bishop Duffy of Clogher. Edmund Murphy himself, already regretting his role as witness against the Primate, was devious in his answers and made a futile attempt to bolt from the hall. When brought back he accused the other witnesses of testifying out of sheer malice and was finally committed to Newgate for contempt of court. John Mac Clave, parish priest of Aughnamullen, Co. Monaghan, claimed to have raised money in his parish for the Primate and to have seen letters from him in France.

The last of the priest witnesses and by far the most hostile to the Archbishop, John Moyer, was the only one to produce documents in court. He read from what he claimed was a copy of a translation of a letter sent by the Archbishop to the secretary of Propaganda in 1672 and from a copy of the decrees of the Synod of Clones (1670) signed in Oliver Plunkett's own hand. Moyer asserted that these were brought from Ireland in 1672 by Niall O'Neill, the young clerical student whom the Primate had sent to study in Rome but who died during his course there. In reply to Moyer's evidence the Archbishop also produced a number of documents meant to destroy Moyer's credibility as a witness. They included two letters written by Moyer to Fr John Anthony O'Neill, Owen Roe's son, in 1678, which showed Moyer's bitter hostility towards the Archbishop.

With the completion of Moyer's evidence the case for the prosecution was for all practical purposes closed. The only remaining witness, Hugh Hanlon of Sturgan in South Armagh, who was married to Niall O'Neill's sister, was called merely to back up what Moyer had said about the Archbishop's letters being brought by O'Neill to Rome.

## The prisoner's defence

As given in the official report of the trial, the Archbishop's defence is disappointing. With his Roman training in Canon Law he might have been expected to cross-examine the witnesses closely and to point out the many contradictions in their evidence. Yet he contented himself with repeatedly protesting against being tried in England and not allowed sufficient time.

A small sheet of paper, $7\frac{1}{4}'' \times 6''$, now preserved in Downside Abbey and still bearing the marks of where it was folded and soiled by the sweat from the Primate's hand, is the only surviving indication that he may have intended to defend himself much more strenuously than the printed record of the trial shows. The reports of the Popish Plot trials which reached

the public were meant to be an *apologia* for the justice
of the verdicts and executions. They were edited by
a well-known Whig supporter and proceeds of the
sales went to Titus Oates himself. In Oliver Plunkett's
case the report was passed for printing by none other
than the Chief Justice. All these factors make one
suspect that anything which might have cast doubt
on the verdict would have been deliberately omitted
in the official printed report of the trial.

The sheet of paper in Downside however suggests
that Oliver brought upwards of a dozen documents
to his trial. It is unlikely that he would not have used
several of them, but the printed version of the trial
includes only a few sentences from two of them. The
others included two documents from the Viceroys,
Berkeley and Essex, papers signed by Edmund
Murphy, letters from Patrick O'Donnelly and Codin
Murphy and several documents concerning John
Moyer. Yet even independent accounts of the trial
comment that the defence was weak.

## Witness for the defence

After the completion of the evidence, the Solicitor-
General summarised the main charges which had been
made by the two Mac Moyers, Duffy and Mac Clave.
He was followed by Jeffreys who joked at the
prisoner's expense and concluded that there was full
proof of every treason laid to the prisoner's charge.
Before the Chief Justice summed up for the jury,
however, a stranger approached the dock and handed

the prisoner a paper containing the names of David Fitzgerald, Eustace Cummins and Paul Gormley who would be prepared to give evidence on his behalf.

When the three names were called, only Paul Gormley answered. He had secured release from prison in Ireland to give evidence about the Popish Plot, but he was not prepared to link the Archbishop with it. He now testified that he had never heard the name of the Archbishop linked with any crime in Ireland and that in his view the Archbishop had done more good than damage there.

This episode was an ill-advised attempt on the part of Oliver's friends outside to provide him with witnesses for the defence. They had stooped to witnesses of the same level as those for the prosecution; of the three whom they suggested only one had turned up and even he had nothing to say. The incident only weakened the Archbishop's genuine grievance that he had not been given sufficient time to bring his witnesses from Ireland.

In his final summing-up to the jury Chief Justice Pemberton made it clear that if they believed the evidence which had been offered by the witnesses they must find the prisoner guilty. The Archbishop contented himself with saying that none of the charges made against him was true "but all plain romance". The jury retired for only a quarter of an hour and when they filed back again the foreman answered that the verdict was "Guilty". "*Deo Gratias*" was the prisoner's only comment.

## Sentence of death

On 15 June 1681 Oliver Plunkett was brought to the bar to receive sentence. Having been asked if he had anything to say why sentence of death should not be pronounced on him, he went over much of the familiar ground again but added the extra bit of information that his witnesses had arrived in Coventry on the previous morning and would be in London in a few days. Pemberton before sentencing him made a strong attack on the Catholic religion which was "the bottom of your treason". The hangman then tied the prisoner's thumbs and the judge donned the black cap before pronouncing the frightening sentence :

> And therefore you must go from hence to the place from whence you came, that is, to Newgate.
> And from thence you shall be drawn through the city of London to Tyburn.
> There you shall be hanged by the neck but cut down before you are dead.
> Your bowels shall be taken out and burnt before your face.
> Your head shall be cut off and your body be divided into four quarters, to be disposed of as his Majesty pleases.
> And I pray God to have mercy on your soul.

From the time that Oliver Plunkett was transferred as a prisoner to London the Catholic world had tried to intervene on his behalf. Pope Innocent

XI had known the Archbishop personally in Rome and as early as December 1680 urged Emperor Leopold to get his ambassador in London to intervene. The good offices of the Spanish ambassador in London and of the Duchess of Modena (mother of the Duchess of York) were also sought. But all to no avail.

In England the persecuted Catholics of London rallied to his side. The Queen and the Duke of York were sympathetic and a score of others (including several titled persons) mentioned by name by the Archbishop in one of his last letters gave him financial assistance. "The English Catholics were here most charitable to me; they spared neither silver nor gold to relieve me," he wrote. Even Essex, despite having thrown in his lot with the opposition against the King, made a last-minute appeal to the King to pardon him. When Essex told Charles that the charges could not possibly be true, the King answered: "Why did you not say that at the trial? It might have done him some good then. I dare pardon no-one. His blood be upon your head, not mine."

## Without fear

Courage had always been one of Oliver Plunkett's outstanding qualities but his calm courage during the last fortnight as he awaited the carrying out of the death sentence amazed even himself. He wrote about it to his former secretary Fr Michael Plunkett, in Rome:

Sentence of death was passed against me on the

15th without causing me any fear or depriving me of sleep for a quarter of an hour. . . . I die most willingly. And being the first among the Irish, I will teach others, with the grace of God, by example, not to fear death. But how am I, a poor creature, so stout, seeing that my Redeemer began to fear, to be weary and sad, and that drops of his blood ran down to the ground? I have considered that Christ, by His fears and passion, merited for me to be without fear.

During that last fortnight the date of his execution was postponed on three occasions. On Saturday 18 June he was told that it would take place on the following Tuesday. When Tuesday came it had been postponed to Friday 24 and he rejoiced that it would be carried out on a Friday and on the Feast of St John the Baptist. It was then put off for another week but he found some consolation in the fact that it would still take place on a Friday and on the Baptist's Octave Day.

After sentence of death had been passed on him the Archbishop was allowed more freedom in Newgate. James McKenna could visit him in private and bring messages from him to the other prisoners and to the outside world. Many Catholics visited him in his cell to receive his blessing. "There appeared," says his fellow-prisoner Fr Maurus Corker, "in his words, in his actions, in his very countenance, something so divinely elevated, such a composed mixture of cheerfulness, constancy, courage, love, sweetness and candour as manifestly denoted the divine goodness had made him fit for a victim and destined him for Heaven. None saw him or came near him but received new comfort, new fervour, new desires to please, serve and suffer for Christ Jesus by his very presence."

## A friend in need

As soon as Oliver was given the "liberty of the prison" in April 1681 he became aware that another of the cells housed a priest. This was Dom Maurus Corker, a Yorkshire convert to the faith, who had become a Benedictine in the Abbey of Lamspringe in Germany but was arrested on his return to England and accused by Titus Oates of involvement in the Popish Plot. Having been sentenced to death and reprieved through the influence of his friends he was imprisoned in Newgate from 1679 on.

While Oliver was still in solitary confinement, Dom Maurus could find out about him only "what I learnt, as it were by chance, from the mouth of the said keepers — that he spent his time in almost continual prayer; that he fasted usually three or four days in a week with nothing but bread; that he appeared to them always modestly cheerful without any anguish or concern at his danger or strict confinement". After the prisoner's arraignment in early May the two were allowed to communicate by letter but as their letters were censored they confined themselves at first to what was essential in preparation for the Archbishop's trial.

From the time 'that Oliver was condemned, how-

ever, James McKenna could bring messages freely
between them, and there developed during the Archbishop's last fortnight on earth a spiritual intimacy
which makes their correspondence one of the most
inspiring chapters in all prison literature. Most of the
Archbishop's other surviving letters are official reports
in Latin or Italian to his superiors in Brussels or Rome,
but in the letters to Maurus Corker, which are in
English, he poured out his heart.

Here are some excerpts from these last letters of
the martyr, which show his amazing composure as the
fatal day approaches:

*16 June 1681* I am obliged to you for the favour
and charity of the £20 and for all your former
benevolence; and whereas I cannot in this country
remunerate you, with God's grace I hope to be
grateful in that kingdom which is properly our
country. . . .

*18 June 1681* . . . I am informed the execution
will be upon Tuesday and I long to be out of all
affairs and to have one full day [and] night to
recollect myself.

*Between 18 and 23 June 1681* . . . Your prayers
I desire and all your brethren. The passage is but
short, yet 'tis dangerous, 'tis from time to eternity.
It can never be re-passed or re-iterated. Your
prayers, I say, I beg and your brethren's. . . .

*23 June 1681* The Captain sent to me Mr Cooper
to tell me that tomorrow sennight the execution
will be. Whereas 'tis not upon St John's day, I am
glad 'tis to be upon his octave and upon a Friday

also. He tells me I will be allowed a priest. I desired it should be you. . . .

*24 June 1681* My man James tells me you are not well, which would be an addition to my afflictions, if I may call them afflictions, they being really comforts and objects of joy . . . being the first of my countrymen in this age who suffered here, I desire to lead the way to others since it is fitting that I should strengthen by my example those others in Ireland whom I have exhorted by word. To exhort others to die stoutly is easy and not difficult, but to instruct them by example and by practice is more efficacious. . . . They might have saved their lives by going overseas but the Irish prelates are resolved rather to die than to forsake their flocks. Forstall of Kildare had departed but that I hindered him, for if the captains will fly, 'tis in vain to exhort the single soldiers to stand in battle. . . .

*Between 25 and 29 June 1681* The authentical intimation is come from the sheriff for Friday. 'Tis fit a sheet for my carcass be prepared, if there will be leave got for to bury it. I desire to know is it fit that I add to my speech how I have been denied the spiritual comfort of a clergyman. . . . Considering what happened and what you know, I think I ought not make any mention of being denied a priest.

*Between 25 and 29 June 1681* . . . I had rather make use of the *Miserere mei Deus* and other prayers of the Church than of any prayers of my own brain's invention. . . . My speech goeth on particulars, which have more force of moving the sense or the ear. . . .

*30 June 1681* (This is the Archbishop's last letter, written on the day before his execution. We give the text of this letter in full with the few Latin phrases translated into English):

Sir,

I do most earnestly recommend myself to your prayers and to the most holy sacrifices of all the noble confessors who are in the prison and to such priests as you are acquainted with and I hope soon to be able to requite all your and their kindness. Above all I recommend myself to the prayers of the holy families of Mr Sheldon and the Lady Stafford's and in general to all the good Catholics in this city whose faith and charity are great. I do recommend to you and to them my most faithful servant James McKenna who served me these eleven years. Some of the good Catholics who came to see me told me that after my death they would be charitable to him. I desire that you be pleased to tell all my benefactors that for all eternity I will be mindful of them and that I will pray for them until they will come where I hope to come soon and then also will thank them in the sight of the supreme Lord. They deserve all praise in this and by God's grace a crown of glory in the next. I doubt not but their faith, charity and good works will be efficacious with Our Saviour and that there will be soon an end of this persecution and that the wickedness of many will soon be made clear. May God's will be done,

and I beseech my Saviour to give all the good
Catholics perseverance in their faith and good
works and to grant me the grace to be tomorrow
where I may pray for them not in a dark manner
but face to face, and be sure that I am and still
will be

Your obliged friend
OLIVER PLUNKETT

Mr Marshall sent me a shift which now and also
tomorrow I wear. I pray you to restore it to him,
for the gentlewoman who gave it did desire it
should accompany me to the place of execution.
For Mr Korker.

These last letters of the Archbishop led Fr Corker
to write of him later: ". . . now it was I clearly
perceived the spirit of God in him, and those lovely
fruits of the Holy Ghost: charity, joy, peace, patience,
etc. transparent in his soul".

Fr Corker met Oliver Plunkett face to face only
once, yet through James McKenna and the gaolers
he was continually in contact with him during his last
days on earth and has left an unforgettable picture of
how the Archbishop spent the dreary hours of solitude
in his cell in prayerful communion with God:

Concerning the manner and state of his prayer,
he seemed most devoted to pathetic sentences taken
out of Scripture, the Divine Office and Missal,
which he made me procure for him three months
before he died. Upon these sentences he let his

soul dilate itself in love. . . . He continually endeavoured to improve himself and advance in the purity of Divine Love and by consequence also in contrition for his past sins, of his deficiency of both of which this humble soul complained to me as the only thing that troubled him.

## Sacerdos in aeternum

In one of the letters quoted above Oliver mentioned how he was denied the spiritual comfort of a priest, yet, as he told Fr Corker, he felt he ought not to mention this in his last speech "considering what happened and what you know". The reference was to Fr Corker's success, presumably by bribing the jailers, in gaining admission to his cell. Not only was Oliver able to go to confession but the Benedictine arranged to have Mass requisites brought to his cell and the Archbishop had the unforeseen joy of being able to say Mass daily for the last week of his life including the morning of his execution. He had celebrated Mass in all kinds of surroundings from the splendour of Rome to the bare walls of Ballybarrack but this was surely the strangest of all, and his Mass-server once again, as on the slopes of Slieve Gullion, in the courtyard of Charlemont and on the hill of Ardpatrick, was the ever-faithful James McKenna.

Having made Fr Corker his *anamchara* during his last days on earth Oliver surrendered his own will even in temporal matters, to the decisions of his spiritual father. The martyr's insistence on this down to the most minute detail made a lasting impression on the Benedictine :

> . . . as he gave up his soul with all its faculties to the conduct of God, so for God's sake he resigned the care and disposal of his body to unworthy me, and this in such an absolute manner that he looked upon himself to have no further power or authority over it.
>
> For an instance of this, the day before he suffered when I sent a barber to trim him, the man asked him if he should leave anything on the upper lip. He answered he knew not how I would have it, and he would do nothing without my order, so that they were forced to send to me before the barber could finish his work.
>
> Another remarkable instance of his strange humility and resignation was that, about an hour before he was carried to execution, being desired to drink a little glass of sack to strengthen his spirits, he answered he was not at his own disposal but mine, and that he must have leave from me before he would either take it or refuse it; whereupon though I was locked up, yet for his satisfaction his man and the keeper's wife came to my chamber and then returning back told him I enjoined it, upon which he readily submitted.
>
> But I neither can nor dare undertake to describe unto you the signal virtues of the blessed martyr. There appeared in him something beyond expression — something more than human.

## The final hours

It is to documents written or preserved by Fr Corker that we must turn for the details of Oliver's last night in the prison:

> The very night before he died, being as it were at heart's ease, he went to bed at eleven of the clock and slept quietly and soundly till four in the morning, at which time his man, who lay in the room with him, awaked him. So little concern had he upon his spirit, or rather had the loveliness of the end beautified the horror of the passage to it.

On arising he said Mass for the last time and exchanged a few final notes with his friend, disposing of his body and the few worldly belongings which he still possessed. The writing on the three notes which bear his signature is firm and bold and shows no trace of nervousness:

> (1) I do acknowledge to have received from Mr Korker what was deposited in his hands for my use, as witness my hand the first of July 1681.
>
> OLIVER PLUNKETT
>
> (2) My body and clothes etc. is at Mr Korker's will and pleasure to be disposed of the first July 81.
>
> OLIVER PLUNKETT
>
> (3) I send you all what I could now and do also send you my blessing.
>
> OLIVER PLUNKETT

The Archbishop was destined to have a companion that morning on the road to Tyburn. He was Edward

Fitzharris, a Wexfordman by birth, spy and forger, whose trial had become a *cause célèbre* because of the House of Commons' attempt to impeach him in Parliament. He was brought from his cell in the Tower and tied to the sledge drawn by horses. Then the procession headed by soldiers moved off in the direction of Newgate where the second victim was waiting.

It must have been about 9 a.m. when Oliver was taken from his cell and brought out to the prison yard to join the procession. Fr Corker caught a last glimpse of him from his cell window and described it afterwards : "When he was carried out of the Priests' Yard to execution he turned about towards our chamber windows and with a pleasant aspect and elevated hand gave us his benediction." Even the Governor of Newgate bore testimony to his calmness, for he reported to the Lieutenant of the Tower: ". . . when I came to him this morning he was newly awake, having slept all night without any disturbance; and when I told him to prepare for his execution, he received the message with all quietness of mind, and went to the sledge as unconcerned as if he had been going to a wedding."

Tyburn was about two miles from Newgate, and over roughly cobbled streets and through growing throngs of people the journey must have taken the best part of an hour. The broad gallows which could hang up to a score at the same time was erected in what is now the centre of the street at Hyde Park corner. In contrast to Fitzharris who had to be helped

up the steps the Archbishop showed no fear as he
mounted the platform and proceeded to address his
"speech from the gallows" to the assembled multitude.

## Last speech

Oliver Plunkett's last speech was printed in London
immediately after his execution and was later translated into several languages including Irish and
Italian. Fr Corker also took the precaution of sending
a signed copy of it for safe keeping to the Spanish
embassy in London. Archbishop John Brenan says
it took an hour to deliver, but to read it at normal
speed requires no more than 15-20 minutes. Some of
the news-sheets on the following day commented on
the length of time which the condemned man spent
speaking and praying, but reaction among the on-
lookers does not seem to have been hostile.

In his speech the Archbishop referred once more
to the short time allowed him to bring witnesses and
documents from Ireland and denied in turn the seven
main accusations made against him at the trial. He
had not, he declared, sent letters to the Continent
by Niall O'Neill nor written the letter quoted by
Moyer nor kept an agent in Rome about civil affairs.
He had not carried on negotiations with France
through Captain Con O'Neill nor collected money
to aid a Spanish or French invasion. He had not
surveyed the ports of Ireland and had only been once
in Carlingford. Finally he had attended no meetings
where there was question of collecting money for sub-

versive purposes or exhorting those who had lost their estates to take up arms.

The Archbishop went on to reveal that a great peer had given him notice in prison that his life would be spared if he would accuse others. This he rejected absolutely. He openly confessed that he had performed the functions of a Catholic bishop in Ireland as long as he was permitted to do so, and had striven, by preaching and canonical regulations, to reform the clergy. He then forgave those priests who had sworn falsely against him and called on his hearers not to condemn the Franciscan Order or the Catholic clergy as a whole because of the misdeeds of a few, for even the Twelve Apostles had a Judas in their number and the seven deacons a Nicholas. He forgave all those who had played a part in his death. He prayed for the King, Queen, Duke of York and royal family. He asked pardon of all those whom he had offended and prayed for forgiveness of his own sins. He then recited the psalm *Miserere,* and as the hangman put the noose around his neck and the cap over his eyes he continued to repeat the invocation: "Into thy hands, O Lord, I commend my spirit" until the horse had pulled the cart from under his feet and he was left dangling by the neck.

At least three priests were near the gallows to give the Archbishop a final absolution: Fr Edward Petre, a Jesuit who was allowed out of prison on parole, Fr Gasper, a Belgian Carmelite attached to the Spanish Embassy and Fr Lucian Travers, an English

Carmelite, who assisted in recovering the dismembered corpse for burial. The body was cut down and quartered, the head severed and the entrails thrown into the blazing fire. The head was also cast into the fire but it was retrieved before the flames could do more than scorch it.

In his last letter to Michael Plunkett in Rome the Archbishop had included a long list of English people who had assisted him during his imprisonment. They included "Mr Sheldon" and "Mr Sheldon's family". Elizabeth Sheldon was at Tyburn on the fatal day, having obtained the King's permission to receive the martyr's remains. With the assistance of McKenna and the three priests she had the remains placed in a large chest and brought from the scene of the execution. A Catholic surgeon named John Ridley removed the two arms at the elbows. The arms were placed in a long tin box and the head in a round tin one, both of which remained in the care of Elizabeth Sheldon until Fr Corker's release from Newgate. The document of authentication of these relics, signed by Elizabeth Sheldon and John Ridley on 29 May 1682, is now preserved in Drogheda. The remainder of the body was coffined and buried in the churchyard of St Giles, not far from the graves of the five Jesuits martyred in 1678.

## Relics and mementos

When Fr Corker was released from prison in 1683, he had the body exhumed, and he removed all the relics to the Benedictine monastery at Lamspringe, not far from Hildesheim in West Germany. Shortly afterwards he brought the martyr's head to Rome and deposited it in the care of Cardinal Howard, who thirteen or fourteen years earlier had received Oliver so hospitably in the King's Palace in Whitehall. After the Cardinal's death it remained with the Dominicans of Santa Sabina until Hugh McMahon, Archbishop of Armagh, received it about 1720. Some years before the latter's death in 1737 he placed it in the care of the Dominican nuns in Drogheda where Mother Catherine Plunkett, a relative of the martyr, was prioress, and the precious relic remained there for nearly two centuries until it was transferred to St Peter's Church, Drogheda, on 29 June 1921.

The remainder of the martyr's body rested for two centuries in a special shrine erected by Fr Corker in the Abbey church of Lamspringe. The abbey was secularised at the beginning of the nineteenth century but it was not until 1883 that Dom Gasquet (afterwards Cardinal) had the relics transferred to Downside Abbey, England. In May 1975 further portions of these relics were brought back from Downside to Ireland.

Other relics and souvenirs of the martyr have found their way to Britain, France, Germany, U.S.A. and even Australia. The Franciscan convent at Goodings near Newbury in Berkshire possesses the left upper arm-bone and other relics. This arm-bone was probably the relic given to Elizabeth Sheldon, Oliver's

great benefactor, and was preserved by the Moning-
tons, a recusant family, at Sarnesfield throughout the
penal times. The left fore-arm came into the possession
of the English Benedictine nuns in Paris in the 1690s
when Dom Maurus Corker was chaplain there but
it seems to have been subsequently lost. The right fore-
arm was entrusted to Archbishop John Brenan, from
whom it passed down through his successors in the
See of Cashel and ultimately came to Dr James
Butler's housekeeper. Much reduced in size by being
used to provide others with small relics of the martyr
it was presented by her to Dr Moran in the nineteenth
century and he handed it over in 1872 to the Dominican Convent, Cabra, where it is still preserved. Small
portions of bone were removed from the shrine in
St Peter's, Drogheda during the 1950s and enshrined
in Boston and Chicago.

A rib taken from the martyr's body before its transfer from Lamspringe to Downside in 1883 was
brought from Lamspringe to Drogheda in 1921 and
is now preserved in the Siena Convent there. It is this
relic which is borne annually in procession through
the streets of Drogheda. The Siena Convent also
possesses the brass plate which marked Oliver's tem-
porary grave in St Giles's churchyard from 1681 to
1683. The heavy oaken door of the Newgate cell
where the Archbishop awaited execution was brought
to Drogheda in 1951 by the Mayor of Wrexham and
is now in St Peter's Church.

Mass vestments belonging to the Archbishop were

preserved until recent times in Killeen Castle, Co. Meath. They were presented by Lord Fingall to Bishop Kyne and are now in the custody of the Bishop of Meath. The martyr's episcopal ring is in the possession of Lord Dunsany. A chalice and thurible belonging to him have found a home in Clonliffe College, Dublin, and portion of another thurible, discovered in the ruins of the penal-day chapel at Ballybarrack where he carried out so many of his ordinations, is now in Maynooth College Museum. A further chalice which belonged to the martyr, together with his watch, were brought to Australia in the nineteenth century and presented to Cardinal Moran of Sydney. They are now deposited in St Patrick's College, Manly.

## Reaction and repentance

Oliver Plunkett was the last victim to suffer death because of the Popish Plot. If he had been granted the extra days for which he pleaded so often, it is almost certain that he would have cheated the hangman. For the tide was already turning against his accusers as he mounted the gallows.

On the very next day Shaftesbury was imprisoned in the Tower and on his release felt his life so threatened in England that he went into exile and died in Holland. Essex was arrested in 1683 and committed suicide in the Tower. By 1685 Titus Oates, once adored as "the saviour of the nation", found himself sentenced to life imprisonment for perjury, and though pardoned later under William III disappeared into obscurity.

Several of the Irish witnesses fared no better than their masters. Henry O'Neill was sentenced to death for robbery and before his execution retracted his evidence against the martyr who was, he said, "altogether innocent of those crimes whereof he was accused and for which he died". Florence Weyer, having suffered a term of imprisonment in Ireland, survived until 1713. His tombstone, often broken and desecrated, was finally lost, and only a heap of stones on which each passer-by cast an extra stone in dishonour is now pointed out as his last resting place in Ballymoyer. Edmund Murphy served two periods of imprisonment in England, worked as a farm labourer in Kent and disappeared from history in poverty in London. Friar John Moyer having been put on trial for his life, sought reconciliation with the Church in 1709, and Rome empowered Bishop O'Donnelly of Dromore to receive him back into the Church. Friar Hugh Duffy survived Oliver Plunkett's death by forty years and in 1721 was inspired to repentance on being shown the head of his victim by Archbishop McMahon.

Of the fate of the other four witnesses, the priest John McClave and the laymen Hugh Hanlon, Phelim O'Neill and Owen Murphy, we have no knowledge — their role in the trial was only a minor one, and even local tradition, usually so persistent a force in the Irish countryside, has long since forgotten their names. Let us hope that, as in the case of the priests mentioned above, the dying Archbishop's prayer from the scaffold *Lord, lay not this sin to them* merited for them all in due course the grace of true repentance.

## Of saintly memory

Immediately after his execution Oliver Plunkett was given the title *martyr* in letters to Rome by Archbishop John Brenan of Cashel and Bishop Forstall of Kildare, by the Benedictine Fr Corker and the Jesuit Fr Teyling. Yet, because, it would seem, of the penal laws, which continued for a further century, no effort was made during the eighteenth century to have his cause examined by Rome. In fact Oliver Plunkett came to be largely forgotten, even in Ireland, throughout the eighteenth century. He was only occasionally mentioned by his successors in Armagh, as when Archbishop Hugh McMahon in his *Jus Primatiale Armacanum* in 1728 referred to him as a "prelate of mild disposition and outstanding holiness who shed lustre on our Church by a glorious martyrdom".

The northern Gaelic poets, though writing in an area which had so many personal associations with the Archbishop and singing the praises of the Plunketts of Rocksavage and the Plunketts of Rathmore, passed over him in silence. Did they still regard him as an outsider in that area where anyone born south of Dundalk was considered in some sense a foreigner? At any rate it was left to Connachtman Seán Ó Neachtain, writing in Dublin, to compose the only verse on Oliver Plunkett which is known to me in the whole corpus of eighteenth-century Gaelic poetry — it is contained in a poem on the imprisonment of Bishop Patrick O'Donnelly in 1708 in which the poet blames Satan for providing false witnesses against O'Donnelly as he had done against Oliver Plunkett:

Nár mheall sé le hiomad óir,
Le gealla fós do bhí ard,
Drongaibh neamhdhílis den chléir
Do chum bréag ar an bpríomháidh?

## Reawakening of interest

Professor George Crolly of Maynooth College was the first nineteenth-century writer to make the salient facts of Oliver Plunkett's life available to a wide reading public. His book, published in Dublin in 1850, was followed a decade later by Moran's *Memoirs of the Most Rev. Oliver Plunket* (1861) which incorporated a great number of the martyr's letters from the Roman archives. Moran's material, though somewhat haphazard in arrangement, has proved a great quarry for all subsequent biographers of the martyr.

The popular biographies by Fleming (1897), who published almost a word for word account of the trial; O'Riordan (1920), unfinished serial in *The Catholic Bulletin*; Concannon (1935), Stokes (1954), Mathews (1961), Curtis (1963) and Forristal (1975) have all added to our knowledge and understanding

of the martyr's life. He has become known to readers
of Italian through the life by Salotti (1920) and to
readers of French through the work of Marie de
Miserey (1963). New information on particular questions connected with him has been made available
through the researches of L. P. Murray (Gaelic background), P. Walsh (family relationships), A. Curtayne
(Trial), C. Mooney (Franciscan connections), J. Brady
(Arrest) and several others. As an indication of the
great interest which was taken in historical research
on Oliver Plunkett during the past few decades, it
may be mentioned that *Seanchas Ard Mhacha,* the
annual journal of the Armagh Diocesan Historical
Society, has carried eighteen articles or shorter items
on him in its fourteen issues. A host of booklets, pam-
phlets, leaflets and several plays, pageants, radio and
television programmes have passed on the latest find-
ings of research workers to the man in the street and
made Blessed Oliver one of the few Irish historical
figures before the nineteenth century whose features
will be recognised immediately by the great majority
of Irish people.

## Movement for canonisation

Exactly a century has now gone by since the first
faint steps were taken which have led ultimately to
the canonisation of Oliver Plunkett. During the 1870s,
after careful scrutiny by the Westminster diocesan
authorities, the first list was submitted to Rome of

those Catholics who had been put to death in England during the centuries of persecution. As London was the place where Oliver had suffered, his name was naturally included in this list, but at the request of the Irish hierarchy Pope Leo XIII signed the decree for the introduction of his cause separately in December 1886.

Much fervent prayer and the untiring efforts of a handful of devoted clients of the martyr (of whom one must single out Mgr Michael O'Riordan, Rector of the Irish College, Rome) went into the thirty-two years' labour which brought the first notable result in 1918. On St Patrick's Day 1918 the Declaration of Martyrdom was finally pronounced in the presence of Pope Benedict XV. Two years later, on Whit Sunday 1920, in the presence of Cardinal Logue, Oliver's fifteenth successor in Armagh, a great concourse of cardinals, bishops and priests and about fifty thousand people, Oliver was solemnly beatified in St Peter's basilica. Ireland rejoiced in the midst of her sorrows as the War of Independence was then at its height; it is noteworthy that the Truce which brought it to an end came into force on the Feast of Blessed Oliver, July 11, 1921.

Yet those who thought that within a few years a new Irish saint would be proclaimed were destined to suffer long years of disappointment. A decade passed without further advance and the League of Prayer for the Canonisation of Blessed Oliver Plunkett was set up in 1933. It initiated a highly successful

campaign lasting many years to spread devotion to
Blessed Oliver, to make his life-story more widely
known, to bring pilgrims to his shrine in Drogheda
and to encourage people to pray urgently for the
miraculous favours required for his canonisation.
Petitions requesting his canonisation were sent to
Rome by the Irish Hierarchy in 1935, by several
cardinals and bishops in European countries, America
and Australia in subsequent years, by 112 members
of the U.S.A. Hierarchy in 1938 and by hundreds
of corporate bodies and individuals among the laity.
The Canonical process was begun in Rome and the
Sacred Congregation sanctioned the appointment of
Mgr Curran, Rector of the Irish College, as Postulator of the cause and Archdeacon Lyons, P.P., St
Peter's, Drogheda, as its Vice-Postulator. Yet it was
only in 1951 that the Sacred Congregation formally
recognised that the evidence submitted by the Postu-
lators justified further investigation.

While Archdeacon Stokes, P.P., St Peter's,
Drogheda, spared no effort during the 1950s to
make Drogheda a national centre of devotion to
Blessed Oliver, the big breakthrough came, not in
Ireland, but in Italy. In April 1958 a certain Signora
Giovanna Marchese of Martirigiano was brought to
the Clinica Mediterranea in Naples suffering from
rupture of the womb. In the operating theatre it was
found that she had developed "incurable necrotic
inflammation of the bladder" and the doctors advised
that she be taken home to die. An Irish Medical

Missionary of Mary, Sister Cabrini Quigley, a native of Donegal who was tragically drowned in the bay of Naples in 1966, prayed frequently during the night to Blessed Oliver for a miraculous cure. Before morning the patient unexpectedly regained consciousness and showed signs of recovery which was maintained thereafter until she was restored to good health.

The next breakthrough came in 1969 after the appointment as Postulator of Mgr John Hanly. In retrospect the conjunction of so many features in an Irish priest resident in Rome must seem almost providential. He was a native of Oldcastle, Co. Meath, the parish in which the martyr's birthplace is situated. He was a historian who had secured his doctorate in Rome for a thesis on Blessed Oliver's pastoral work. His appointment as Postulator coincided with the third centenary of Blessed Oliver's appointment to Armagh in 1669. At home in Ireland, under the inspiration of Cardinal Conway, the Blessed Oliver Plunkett Crusade was set up and with a young and enthusiastic batch of diocesan directors at the helm the annual July pilgrimage to Drogheda drew over ten thousand pilgrims. The Cardinal announced that the objective now was the canonisation of the martyr within the next few years and at least before the third centenary of his death in 1981.

The new Postulator decided to go all out to secure acceptance of the Naples cure. The Process investigating it began in June 1969 and did not conclude until 1972. Its *acta* were then submitted to the Sacred

Congregation for the Causes of the Saints in Rome. In turn the medical and theological aspects of the miracle were approved. Rome was then petitioned to dispense with the need for a second miracle as had been done in the case of the Forty English and Welsh Martyrs in 1970. When this petition was granted, the road was open to early canonisation. With unbounded gratitude to God and to all those who down the years had laboured for the cause, Ireland heard that Blessed Oliver would be canonised in St Peter's Rome, on Sunday, 12 October 1975. It was now the turn of the Irish people to say, as Oliver had said on receiving the verdict of the court: *Deo Gratias.*

# Epilogue

## Oliver : the man and the saint

More than two hundred of Oliver Plunkett's letters survive but only rarely does one glimpse his personality through what is largely a series of official reports.

Tall, erect, handsome, his shoulder-length wig and well-trimmed beard and moustache framed a face of great strength with eyes at once penetrating and compassionate. Spectacles obtained in London in January 1670 did not cure an ailment which made his eyes run when exposed to the elements. Never of robust constitution, he aged prematurely and before his death was "subject to divers infirmities" of which the most troublesome was "the distemper of the stone and gravel which often afflicts him".

During his first months as Primate a sword and wig and pistols served to disguise him as "Captain Browne", who allayed suspicions by singing in taverns and kissing the ladies. Thereafter he wore cheap frieze, spurning the *lavidensa* favoured by some clerics, to save money for more pressing purposes. To the same end he ate only plain fare, having on many occasions "nothing to eat but oaten bread, salty butter and stirabout and nothing to drink but milk".

Highly intelligent and well-read (even in prison he could quote six lines of Boethius from memory) he threw himself into his episcopal duties with reforming zeal and unflagging energy. Yet his letters reveal a quiet sense of humour unusual in a reformer.

Of his physical and moral courage there can be no question. If he stayed in Rome in 1654, he stood firm in Ireland in 1673-74 and again in 1678-79, resolved never to depart unless "dragged to the ship". Unyielding in controversy, even to the point of exaggeration, his judgment of men and motives was sometimes faulty and could change suddenly. He inspired undying love and consuming hate: the loyalty of James McKenna and the hostility of John Moyer. Even his best friend John Brenan found him touchy and hot-tempered. He inherited from his forebears a family pride which placed great store on nobility of birth and could never allow a Plunkett to yield to a Talbot. But he inherited also their passion for good order, civilised living and peace.

*Gratia praesupponit et perficit naturam.* The long months of solitary confinement revealed a new Oliver, tested like gold in the furnace. His unyielding courage had become a calm serenity before martyrdom. His deep humanity had been transformed into a tenderness which embraced all men. He had soared above the struggles of this world and could face death with the clear vision of a saint whose eyes were fixed on eternity.

# Appendix

## Places associated with Oliver Plunkett

Loughcrew, the birthplace of Oliver Plunkett, is situated a few miles south-east of Oldcastle, Co. Meath, just below the cairn-topped hills of Sliabh na Caillí. A pleasant "yew-walk" which according to tradition was planted by the Plunketts leads from its square-towered pre-Reformation church to a splendidly preserved Norman motte. Beyond are the remains of an old mill. A corn mill stood on the property of John Plunkett of Loughcrew, Oliver's father, in 1640. Much of the land is still owned by the Napper family who displaced the Plunketts at the Cromwellian Plantation, and the present Napper residence is near the family's former "big house", a Palladian mansion which was destroyed by fire. Loughcrew is now in the Catholic parish of Oldcastle whose fine Gothic church is to receive a major relic of the martyr in this year of his canonisation.

North Louth contains most of the landmarks associated with Oliver's decade as Primate. The tiny churches of Ballybarrack, a short mile south of Dundalk, and Ardpatrick on a hill overlooking the village of Louth, have been aptly called his pro-cathedrals.

Nothing but a grassy mound was visible at Bally-barrack until the early years of the present century. Excavations laid bare the four walls of the church, fifty feet long by seventeen wide, to a height of four feet, together with two doorways and a stone altar. The only ecclesiastical object found in the debris was the top of a thurible with Celtic tracery pronounced to be sixteenth century work. Oliver's dwellinghouse on his return to Ireland was in the same parish—he described his room as "scarce seven feet high, its roof of thatch". It is appropriate that Blackrock in this parish should have erected the first church dedicated to Oliver half a century ago.

Oliver's second "pro-cathedral" was at Ardpatrick, a splendid hill-site deriving its name from St Patrick himself. Here the Primate was on land belonging to his distant cousin, Oliver Plunkett, Baron of Louth, who at the Restoration recovered part of his estates including "the lands of Ardpatrick, 103 acres". In 1672 Lord Louth leased Ardpatrick to Stephen Taaffe of Dowanstown, and it was probably at this time that the Archbishop took up residence there.

The ruins of Ardpatrick church were completely hidden until 1935, when excavations revealed a struc-ture similar to Ballybarrack, about thirty feet long by fifteen feet wide, with the walls still standing to a height of about four feet and a stonebuilt altar at the eastern end. One marvels at how three bishops and nine other ecclesiastics fitted comfortably within the walls in 1678.

Local tradition still points out the site of the Archbishop's house near the garden wall of the present Ardpatrick House. The latter however was not built until the eighteenth century. Not far from the house stands a centuries-old oak tree, still called "Blessed Oliver's oak" or "Blessed Oliver's Bed", where according to tradition he often sought refuge from his pursuers.

The Archbishop brought his brother Edward and the latter's family to reside with him at Ardpatrick. Edward is described as "Edward Plunkett of Loughcrew or Ardpatrick" in Archdall's edition of Lodge's *Peerage*. He had become mentally afflicted before the Archbishop's death. His family consisted of three boys and two girls; it is only by assuming that they were living with the Archbishop, who was helping with their lessons, that one can explain the warmth and tenderness of his references to them in one of his last letters before execution: ". . . also my nephews and nieces. Jemmy and Joseph begun their philosophy and Nicky ended his prosody. Catty and Tomasin and all will be in a sad condition".

Other places in North Louth associated with Oliver Plunkett are Castletown Castle and Louth Hall. The Primate refers in some of his letters to his visits to the residence of Sir John Bellew at Castletown, now incorporated into the convent of the Sisters of St Louis. Sir John cooperated with the Archbishop in his efforts to persuade the Tories to go abroad and there is some evidence that Patrick Fleming and his party were on their way to Castletown when they were murdered near Iniskeen. In Louth Hall, the residence of Oliver's cousin Lord Louth, he had the use of a secluded room and hid in the ice-house surrounded by a dense plantation of laurels. These traditions concerning his visits to his cousin's mansion have been handed down in unbroken line by a succession of gardeners who worked at Louth Hall.

Passing over the border from North Louth into South Armagh we are following closely the route taken by the Archbishop with Bishop John Brenan when they went on their keeping in the midst of a violent blizzard in the winter of 1673-74. Although Oliver's letters written from his *locus refugii* do not reveal where he was in hiding, a strong and constant tradition has always maintained that it was in the Mullabawn valley under the shadow of Slieve Gullion. A few excerpts from Oliver's letters during the winter show the straits to which he was reduced:

*12 November 1673* "... I shall retire to some little hut in the woods or mountains of my diocese with a supply of candles and books. You can go on sending me letters as usual, however, and I shall try to send you some information from time to time. ..."
*December 1673* "... I am in hiding and Dr Brenan is with me. ... I sometimes find it hard even to get oaten bread, and the house where Dr Brenan and I are staying is made of straw and covered or thatched so badly that we can see the

stars when we are in bed, and even the lightest shower of rain sprinkles our pillows. But we are determined to die from hunger and cold rather than desert our flocks. . . ."

*27 January 1674* ". . . There was a biting north wind blowing into our faces and it beat the snow and hail so fiercely into our eyes that even now we are scarcely able to see with them. Many times we were in danger of being lost in the valleys and of dying of suffocation in the snow. . . . The cold and the hail were so terrible that my eyes have not yet stopped running nor have those of my companion. I feel that I shall lose more than one tooth, they are paining me so much, and my companion was attacked with rheumatism in one arm and can scarcely move it. . . ."

Oliver's first period "on the run" lasted until well into 1675. Many places are still pointed out in local tradition as his hiding-places: caves at Killeavy and Faughart, the cairn on the top of Slieve Gullion, the Cadgers' Pass—a mountain path leading from Ravensdale to Omeath—, a grove at Forkhill, a secluded spot near Lislea and areas as far away from his base as North Antrim and East Donegal.

One place in South Armagh whose association with the Archbishop is based on written documents is Dorsey in the parish of Creggan Lower which in the seventeenth century possessed a famous inn run by George Blyke. Its site is still pointed out in the haggard of the farmhouse now occupied by the Burns family on the old coach-road from Dundalk to Armagh. Here the Archbishop often presided at conferences of his northern clergy. The new church built in Dorsey in 1956 is dedicated to him.

Some of the Archbishop's letters are signed from Armagh itself. He commented on the flat countryside with its orchards in the north of the county as compared with the hilly terrain to the south where large herds of pigs and horses were a common sight. He passed by Charlemont Fort across the Blackwater into Co. Tyrone. He visited the Armagh Franciscan Community in its *locus refugii* in Brantry in South Tyrone and was impressed by the large public chapel in which the friars sang Mass and wore their habits. He visited Dungannon to administer confirmation and Castlecaulfield, the residence of the Earl of Charlemont.

In September and October 1670 Oliver journeyed through Down and Connor and sent a very detailed account to Rome of this area and its clergy. He spent three days with the Marquis of Antrim in his castle at Dunluce, planning to visit the Hebrides which had been entrusted to him by Propaganda. But scarcity of money and the danger that he would be suspected of fomenting opposition to the proposed union between England and Scotland caused him to postpone his plan indefinitely.

During the winter of 1670-71, Oliver journeyed to Derry to effect the removal of the Vicar Apostolic

Terence O'Kelly and then moved into Raphoe. Here he made the acquaintance of Captain John Hamilton, a Catholic convert of planter stock, who accompanied him on his visitation and with whom he often lodged later.

By April 1671 Oliver had visited all the northern dioceses with the exception of Ardagh and Clonmacnois. In July 1671 he was off on his travels again, visiting his own diocese and Down, Dromore and Clogher in connection with the Franciscan-Dominican dispute. It was his only visit to Carlingford and he stayed but half an hour. In September 1671 he again carried out a visitation of Armagh and Raphoe. He travelled to Ardagh in the summer of 1672 to settle the dispute there concerning the appointment of Gerard Farrell as Vicar Apostolic.

It is more difficult to follow Oliver from place to place during the second half of the decade. We do know, however, that he spent June and July 1678 in visitation of the diocese of Armagh. After the Synod of Ardpatrick in August 1678, he began a new visitation of Meath and Clonmacnois which continued until the order was issued in December 1678 commanding all bishops to leave Ireland.

In his speech from the scaffold Oliver stated explicitly that he was never in Cork, Kinsale, Bantry, Youghal or Dungarvan. For thirty-six years he had not been in Limerick, Duncannon or Wexford, a statement which suggests that he had last visited them, in the company of Scarampi, in 1645. He visited Tuam in

February and March 1673 and proceeded to the city of Galway where he was impressed by the fine public churches possessed by the religious orders, particullarly the Dominicans. On this journey west he also visited the diocese of Elphin and met the Bishop of Clonfert. In the autumn of 1676 he travelled to Munster where he was struck by the poverty of clergy and laity. He visited Cashel and spent a month with his old friend John Brenan in the diocese of Waterford.

Apart from an occasional trip to Dublin by mailcoach, Oliver's journeys throughout Ireland were carried out on horseback. In addition to his servant James McKenna he kept at least one stable-boy to look after his horse. One would like to know something of his prowess as a horseman and of the long weary days which he spent in the saddle. His progress in the more remote parts of the country must have been infuriatingly slow for a man who seemed always in a hurry. Yet he visited all four provinces at some stage during his primacy and was so often "on the road" throughout his own diocese and province that there must be few places in Ulster or North Leinster which were not hallowed by the footsteps of Ireland's new Saint.

*The author is deeply indebted to Mgr John Hanly who made available to him the full text and his English translations of Oliver's letters.*

# Part II

## Oliver Plunkett
## In His Own Words

### Desmond Forristal

# 1. IN HIS OWN WORDS

About Oliver Plunkett we have a great mass of information, yet we sometimes feel we hardly know the man at all. The events of his life are recorded in minute detail in the writings of his time but the personality of the man behind the events remains frustratingly elusive.

The reason is simple enough. Nearly all our information about Oliver comes from official sources, from reports, state papers, legal records, Church documents. They give us many facts but little enough of the human background to the facts. In all the countless references to the Archbishop there is not one that gives us a description of his physical appearance, his voice, his accent, his manner of speaking or of moving, or any of the other personal traits and mannerisms that must have been so obvious to his contemporaries but are hidden from later generations.

Neither do we have anything like a convincing character-sketch from any of those who knew him. There is praise and blame of him in plenty, but the one must be regarded with as much caution as the other. Much of the praise is of a conventional sort, especially that written after his death when he was already beginning to take on the aura of a martyr and the writers seemed more concerned with edifying their readers than recording their exact impressions. There is the same lack of reality about the adverse opinions, which generally show obvious malice and are aimed at justifying the writer for his part in some long forgotten dispute with the Archbishop. It is only occasionally that one comes across an impression or an incident that seems to suggest a real man with the good and bad qualities of a real man and not a stylised saint or villain.

To paint his portrait, this book relies mainly upon the man's own words. Fortunately, Oliver Plunkett was an indefatigable letter-writer and, equally fortunately, many of these letters have been preserved. During his active years as Archbishop of Armagh he corresponded continually with the Vatican, reporting on all his activities and on the state of the Irish Church. These letters, still preserved in the Roman archives, are the main source of our information about him and about the Catholic Church in Ireland in the sixteen-seventies.

Yet here again we are doomed to disappointment if we expect any intimate personal revelations, for this was an official correspondence. It was the area representative reporting back to head office, and the facts and figures were what mattered, not the feelings of the writer. No-one wears his heart upon his sleeve when writing to an official he may never even have met. In addition, Oliver was inhibited by the suspicion that his letters were being opened and read by Dublin Castle on their way to Rome, a suspicion which later proved to be only too well founded. Nevertheless, between the lines we get an occasional glimpse of the personality of the writer, all the more authentic in that it is unwittingly given us.

One small group of letters falls into a category of its own. These are the letters which he wrote in his prison cell during the two weeks before his death. Two of these were written to a young kinsman in Rome, the remainder to a Benedictine monk who was his fellow-prisoner in Newgate. In these letters, for the first and only time that we know of, he opened his mind and heart fully in writing to another person. From these faded documents, through their quaint old-fashioned language, there comes to us across a gap of three centuries the truest picture we have of Oliver Plunkett, written in his own words.

## 2. BOYHOOD AND PRIESTHOOD

Oliver Plunkett was born on the 1st of November, 1625, at Loughcrew, near Oldcastle in County Meath. His father was John Plunkett, Baron of Loughcrew, and his mother was born Thomasina Dillon, grand-daughter of Sir Luke Dillon. Oliver came of an aristocratic family in an age when aristocracy meant not just prestige but power and wealth. In Ireland as in every other country of Europe there was a sharp dividing line between the great mass of the people, the peasants and the artisans, and the few noble families who kept all the reins of influence in their small circle and who married their sons and daughters to one another until everybody was related to everybody else. A testimonial letter from the Rector of the Irish College in Rome described Oliver as being "of Catholic parentage, descended from an illustrious family: on the father's side from the most illustrious Earls of Fingal and on the mother's side from the most illustrious Earls of Roscommon, and also connected by birth with the most illustrious Oliver Plunkett, Baron of Louth, first Nobleman of the Diocese of Armagh"; and the information was obviously provided by Oliver himself. He might have come from an obscure corner of an obscure land but the blood of noble forbears flowed in his veins. He was human enough to take pride in the fact and wise enough to take advantage of it in a good cause.

Oliver was one of a family of five, with an elder brother, Edward, and three younger sisters, Catherine, Anne and Mary. His boyhood was an untroubled one: it was a relatively peaceful period in Ireland and the laws against Catholics were not rigidly enforced. In any event, Oliver's family connections protected him both against religious discrimination and the poverty that gripped the vast majority of his fellow-countrymen. They also solved the problem of his education, and his parents naturally thought of Dr Patrick Plunkett, a first cousin of Oliver's mother, when the question of his schooling came up.

Patrick Plunkett was the first great formative influence of Oliver's life and he supervised the boy's education from childhood until his sixteenth year. When he first received the youngster into his household, Patrick was aged about thirty and was acting parish priest in Kilcloon in County Meath. A few years later he was appointed Abbot of St Mary's in Dublin, and later still was to be Bishop successively of Ardagh and of Meath. We have no record of the course of studies which Oliver followed under his guidance but it is clear that the older man made a profound impression on his young pupil. In after years Oliver always spoke of him with great respect and affection.

It was on Patrick Plunkett's advice that Oliver
decided to go to Rome to study for the priesthood.
In 1641 the Ulster rebellion put an end to the
peace of the country and to Oliver's education.
The movement sparked off in Ulster spread rapidly
and led, the following year, to the formation of the
Confederation of Kilkenny, a kind of parliament
which had the support not only of the native Irish
but of the Anglo-Irish gentry as well. Among the
Plunketts who made their way to Kilkenny was
Patrick, taking his place among the Lords Spiritual
in the new parliament. It was evident that he could
no longer continue as Oliver's tutor and anyhow
the boy had now reached the stage where he
needed a more formal and structured education.
The war-torn Ireland of the sixteen-forties could
not offer such an education. The Irish College in
Rome could.

About Oliver's reasons for choosing the priesthood we know little. The staunch faith of his own
parents and home must certainly have been one
factor, the example of Patrick Plunkett another,
and perhaps more powerful one. As the younger
son, he had no rights or responsibilities in regard to
the family estates and the choice of his career was
left to his own judgment. He chose the priesthood,
and having made his choice he followed it with the
tenacity and singleness of purpose that were to be
so characteristic of him in later life. Obstacles
existed only in order to be overcome.

The obstacles that lay between Oliver and Rome
were forbidding enough. Even in peacetime, a
journey to Rome was a formidable undertaking.

Ships often waited weeks in port for a favourable wind and even when at last sea-borne had to run the danger both of storms and of pirates. Land travel was almost as uncertain, with muddy roads, flooded rivers, and bandits lurking in every wood and mountain valley. To these normal hazards, there was now the added complication of war. Ireland was an armed camp, England was a battlefield between Royalists and Puritans, Northern Europe was still in the grip of the Thirty Years War.

It was not until 1646 that an opportunity presented itself. Father Peter Scarampi had been sent by the Pope as an envoy to the Confederation of Kilkenny. Towards the end of 1646, his mission accomplished, he was returning to Rome and had chartered a ship from Waterford. He offered to take with him some students for the Irish College and a group of five suitable young men was assembled in Waterford in December of that year. Oliver Plunkett was one of them. Another was John Brennan, later Archbishop of Cashel, who was to become Oliver's constant companion and closest friend to the end of his life.

As usually happened with Oliver, the winds proved unfavourable. It was not until the 12th of February, 1647, that the ship could leave Waterford. The dangers from pirates and storms still remained to be faced and both duly made their appearance; fortunately for the travellers, they appeared at the same time. On the morning of the second day they spied two larger vessels bearing down on them with hostile intent. The sailors crowded on every stitch of canvas but it soon became clear that the enemy ships were gaining on them, and by nightfall they were only a short distance away.

Father Scarampi and his young companions joined in prayer for deliverance from their pursuers and promised to go in pilgrimage to the shrine of St Francis in Assisi if they escaped. During the night a violent storm blew up and continued for the following two days. The ship was tossed around by mountainous seas and the young men making their first voyage must have longed to feel the firm ground of Ireland beneath their feet again. On the third day, however, the storm blew itself out, the wind died down and the sea calmed. The ship had been blown many miles off its course but the two enemy vessels had disappeared and were not sighted again for the remainder of the voyage.

On the 4th of March they landed at Ostend and set out for Paris. Their troubles were not yet over. In Flanders they fell into the hands of a band of robbers who took all their valuables and held them to ransom. Somehow or other, the ransom was paid and the travellers resumed their journey. Passing through Paris and Lyons, they entered Italy and made first for Assisi to fulfil their promise to St Francis. It was well into the month of May when they finally entered Rome. The journey from Ireland had taken three months; if one takes into account the delay in Waterford, five months.

Like many an Irishman before him and after him, Oliver grew to love Rome and feel very much at home there. After the turmoil of his native country, the peace and order of the City were all the more striking to the young man. The contrast between the splendour of the Church in Rome and its poverty in Ireland was especially noticeable. In the recently completed Basilica of St Peter's, the Pope presided over the solemn ceremonies in golden vestments, and the finest painters, sculptors, and composers of the day were employed to give greater magnificence to the liturgy. Bernini, greatest of all baroque architects, was at the height of his powers and new churches designed by him and his disciples were adding new glory to the city. To wander through the streets of Rome, to visit the Colosseum and the catacombs, to watch the old buildings being demolished and the new ones taking their place, merely to stand and see people of many nationalities passing by, was a heady experience for the young Irishman and one that he never forgot.

The news that continued to come from Ireland during Oliver's student days made the difference between the two countries more cruelly apparent than ever. By 1649 the Confederation of Kilkenny had broken up in disorder and Cromwell and his army had landed in Ireland to mop up what resistance still remained. His first and most spectacular act of vengeance was against the city of Drogheda, on the border of Oliver's native county. The entire garrison of more than two thousand men were put to the sword and when some of the defenders took refuge in St Peter's Church Cromwell ordered that the building be burnt around them. Many civilians died, and priests and friars were hunted down with particular ferocity. It was, wrote Cromwell, a "righteous judgment of God upon these barbarous wretches, who have imbrued their hands in so much innocent blood". During the years that followed, Cromwell and his lieutenants continued to wreak God's righteous judgment upon the barbarous Irish. One after another, the Irish towns fell to the invaders, the last in 1652. Everywhere churches were burnt, monasteries scattered, bishops and priests killed or exiled or imprisoned.

What the sword began the law completed. The final stage in Cromwell's plan was the replacing of Irish Catholics by English Protestants. The natives were to lose all their lands in Munster, Leinster and Ulster and remove themselves to the inhospitable wastes of Connaught. Among those who lost all their property was Oliver's elder brother, who had succeeded to the estate on the death of their father. By the end of 1653 Cromwell felt that he had at last found the final solution to the Irish problem.

On the 1st of January, 1654, Oliver Plunkett was ordained priest in Rome. He had been an excellent student, intelligent, studious and devout; the rector of the Irish College later described him as "a model of gentleness, integrity and piety". Now, in accordance with the vow taken by all students of the College, he was to return to Ireland. It was not a cheering prospect, and on the 14th of June he wrote to the Jesuit General asking to be dispensed from his vow. The letter was written in Latin and is the earliest of his writings still preserved for us.

> I, Oliver Plunkett, your most humble peti-
> tioner, student of the Irish College, having
> completed my philosophical and theological
> studies, in view of the impossibility (well known
> to your Paternity) of my now returning to
> Ireland as demanded by the rules of the College
> and the oath I have taken, do humbly request of
> you, Most Reverend Father, that I may be
> allowed to remain in Rome and reside with the
> Fathers of San Girolamo della Carità. I promise,
> however, and declare that I will be always ready
> to return to Ireland whenever you, Reverend
> Father, or my superiors shall so command.

No doubt Oliver was only following standard
practice in writing this request: his friend, John
Brennan, also remained in Rome and there is no
evidence that any of his fellow-students returned
home at this period. No doubt, too, his chances of
getting safely into Ireland were slight: the ports
were watched and there were spies everywhere. Yet
one would like to feel certain that Oliver made his
request only with reluctance, that it took days and
perhaps weeks of argument on the part of friends
and superiors to convince him that his duty lay in
Rome and not among his own people. It would
certainly have been difficult for him to return to
Ireland but it would not have been impossible. But
to a young man of Oliver's ability Rome offered an
attractive and honourable career while Ireland held
out only the prospect of imprisonment and death.
In these circumstances it was easy enough for

him to decide that the prudent course and the course most agreeable to God's will was for him to stay in Rome. He may have been right in that decision but he can hardly have been particularly proud of it. In the years that followed he may have wondered how much fear mingled with the prudence and how he would bear himself if ever called upon to choose between his life and his principles. It was not until his last days on earth that these doubts were to be finally laid to rest.

Meanwhile, Oliver's ecclesiastical career proceeded smoothly on its course. He continued his studies, attending the lectures on Canon and Civil Law given by Mariscotti, and in due course obtained his doctorate in these two subjects. In 1657 he was appointed Professor of Theology in Propaganda College and was later appointed a Consultor of the Congregation of the Index. He also became active as the agent of the Irish clergy in their dealings with the Vatican. The death of Cromwell in 1658 and the restoration of King Charles II had brought about an easing of the situation in Ireland. The clergy found Oliver always ready to use his influence with the Roman Congregations on behalf of his Irish friends.

Of his private life during the same period less is known. Writing after Oliver's death and when he had already begun to take on the martyr's aura, the Italian writer Marangoni described his life at San Girolamo in these words:

Here it is incredible with what zeal he burned for the salvation of souls. In the house itself and in the city he wholly devoted himself to devout exercises; frequently did he visit the sanctuaries steeped with the blood of so many martyrs and he ardently sighed for the opportunity of sacrificing himself for the salvation of his countrymen. He moreover frequented the hospital of Santo Spirito and employed himself even in the most abject ministrations, serving the sick poor to the edification and wonder of the very officials and assistants of that place.

This is Italian hagiography at its most voluptuous. The picture of Oliver sighing ardently around the tombs of the martyrs in his desire to die for his countrymen is hard to take seriously, especially when we remember the efforts he had recently been making to avoid doing precisely that. Yet Marangoni was a reputable historian and beneath the verbiage there must be a foundation of truth. Perhaps Oliver was still troubled by his decision to opt for the peace of Rome, still uneasily aware that men were fighting and suffering in the front line while he pushed a pen at staff headquarters.

It may have been partly a desire to share in the hardships of the active troops that led Oliver to undertake spare-time work in the hospitals. This part of Marangoni's description is corroborated by a letter of Oliver's in which he speaks of his friend Monsignor Odescalchi, who later became Pope Innocent XI. "I often assisted him when he tended the poor and ragged and needy, many of them covered with vermin. He gave them shelter and clothing at his own expense, he washed and fed

them with his own hands." It is an unexpected
occupation for the Professor of Theology and
second son of the Baron of Loughcrew, and it
shows a side of Oliver's character that we have not
seen before.

## 3. THE NEW ARCHBISHOP

At the beginning of the year 1669 there was only one Catholic bishop active in Ireland, none other than Oliver's durable kinsman, Patrick Plunkett, who that year was transferred from Ardagh to the more prosperous diocese of Meath. The only other bishop in the country was an invalid, the Bishop of Kilmore, "continually infirm in body and occasionally in mind" according to Bishop Plunkett. Three others, including the Archbishop of Armagh, Edmund O'Reilly, were living in exile. The Church in Ireland was recovering from the Cromwellian persecution but recovery was bringing its own problems. The clergy were divided into several quarrelling factions and the lack of a resident hierarchy made it difficult to settle these disputes and restore ecclesiastical discipline.

Accordingly, the Roman authorities decided to appoint new bishops to a number of vacant sees. Dr Peter Talbot, a close friend of the reigning monarch, Charles II, was appointed Archbishop of Dublin. New archbishops were also appointed to Tuam and Cashel and a new bishop to Ossory. Then news arrived in Rome that the Archbishop of

Armagh had died in France, leaving vacant the most important see in Ireland. The choice of his successor would obviously be of crucial importance to the future of the Irish Church.

Immediately the lobbying began. The new Archbishop of Dublin sent in a list of three names and added some unkind remarks about the clergy of Armagh. The clergy of Armagh did nothing to improve their image by writing to threaten uproar if an outsider and particularly a Meath man were appointed to their diocese. Oliver himself, the most obvious candidate for the position, at first let it be known that he wished to remain on in Rome and complete some books he was working on. Later he changed his mind or was persuaded to change his mind and formally put forward his name.

The meeting of the Congregation of Propaganda which was to make the appointment was held on the 9th of July. The Pope himself, Clement IX, was present. After an indecisive discussion about the names proposed by Dr Talbot, all of whom were unsuitable for one reason or another, the Pope impatiently cut short the proceedings. It was a waste of time, he said, to talk about candidates of doubtful suitability when they had in Rome a man who was certainly fitted in every way for the position. That man was Oliver Plunkett.

The announcement of his appointment was greeted with a chorus of praise, led by Archbishop Talbot. Only the clergy of Armagh remained silent, stunned by the imposition of a Meath man upon their diocese. Meanwhile preparations were put in hand for the consecration of the new Primate. The

Roman authorities thought it unwise to provoke the English government by too much publicity; so it was decided that Oliver should leave Rome quietly for Belgium, where he would be consecrated in a private ceremony, and from there make his way to Ireland.

Before leaving Rome, Oliver paid a last visit to the Hospital of Santo Spirito. Father Mieskow, the Superior, said to him: "Monsignor, you are now going to shed your blood for the Catholic faith." The Archbishop-elect answered: "I am not worthy of that; but pray for me that my desire for it may be fulfilled." The story comes from Marangoni, who relates it with the customary embellishments: but as he adds the name of an eye-witness, it is probably substantially true.

Before he had even set foot in Ireland, the new Archbishop had begun the long series of reports and letters to Rome which give us so much information about his activities during the next ten years. His journey to Belgium had been comparatively uneventful and his consecration had taken place according to plan in the private chapel of the Bishop of Ghent, on the 1st of December. He then made his way to London and from there wrote on the 30th of that month to Cardinal Barberini in Rome. The Queen he refers to is Catherine of Braganza, wife of Charles II, who was a Catholic and was allowed by the terms of her marriage treaty to maintain a chapel and priests to serve in it.

I presented Your Eminence's letters to the Queen, who gave me a very gracious audience and spoke highly of you for the affection you have always shown for her and the King and entire nation. She added that those sent by you have always been well-disposed to His Majesty and she hoped for the same from me. I spoke with some of the King's intimates and they told me that he often refers to Your Eminence with affection and regard.

I also delivered your letter to Father Howard, the Grand Almoner, a truly worthy man. He secretly let me stay with him for ten days in his own apartments in the Royal Palace. He also very kindly brought me out driving on several occasions in his carriage to see the principal sights of the city. . . .

It is so cold here at the moment that the Spanish wine actually froze in my chalice. They have not had as bad a winter as this for many years. After the frost there was a heavy fall of snow so that it will be morally impossible to travel until the cold spell is over.

I am not at all anxious, however, to stay on in London in view of the attitude of the Court. The followers of Walsh, or more likely Walsh himself, keep sending anonymous letters to the Ministers of Court, filled with lying stories about what I am doing here; but their ill-will is well known and they themselves are regarded with contempt. One letter to the King said that Father Howard had three hundred priests hidden in the Royal Palace who went around every night trying to make converts for the Pope. One good thing about these stories is they are so far-fetched that no-one believes their authors even when they happen to tell the truth.

It was not until March that Oliver arrived in Ireland, after an absence of twenty-three years. The journey from Rome to Dublin had taken nearly seven months of weary winter travel but the warmth of the welcome that greeted him atoned for a lot. Various noble Plunketts hastened to congratulate the Archbishop on this new honour to their family. Among those he was most glad to see were Bishop Patrick Plunkett, his old friend, and the Bishop's brother, Sir Nicholas Plunkett. He wrote to Rome to report his arrival.

> I arrived in this city at long last on Monday. I can say that I suffered more on the journey from London to Holyhead, where I took the boat, than on all the journey from Rome to London put together. Extreme cold, stormy winds, and heavy snow: and then when the thaw set in, the rivers rose so high with the floods that three times I was up to my knees in water in the carriage. At Holyhead the winds were against me and I had to wait for twelve days. Finally, after a ten hours' journey by sea, I arrived in port here, where the welcomes and the greetings of my friends lessened my sorrow at having had to leave Rome.
>
> Sir Nicholas Plunkett immediately invited me to his house and put his carriage at my disposal. The Earl of Fingall, who is my cousin, invited me to his country seat. The Baron of Louth has offered me board and lodging in my own diocese as long as I please and I have decided to accept

his invitation as he lives in the centre of my area. There are also three other knights who are married to three cousins of mine and who are vying with one another to see which of them can receive me into his house.

I was also delighted to find the Bishop of Meath so well and so fresh. Though he is sixty-eight years old, he looks no more than fifty and has hardly a grey hair in his head. . . .

I made the journey in spite of the bad weather because I wanted to be in my province to begin my duties during Lent. I shall find it difficult to assemble five priests when consecrating the Holy Oils during Holy Week, when all the priests are busy hearing confessions: so I would ask your Excellency to obtain for me the privilege of consecrating the Holy Oils with the assistance of two priests only.

Oliver Plunkett entered his province and his diocese during the Lent of 1670. He was now Archbishop of the diocese of Armagh, Metropolitan of the nine dioceses of the Armagh Province, and Primate of All Ireland. He had the ordinary powers of a bishop within his own diocese, a more limited power in the other dioceses of his province, and a very shadowy jurisdiction over the whole country by virtue of his primacy. His ecclesiastical powers were extensive but ill-defined and the effort to define them more accurately was to teach him many a bitter lesson. The clear distinctions and definitions he had learnt from Canon Law in Rome had a habit of melting away among the mists of the Irish countryside.

The nobility greeted him with joy, the clergy with sullen resentment. Neither side knew much about him after his long absence in Rome except that he was a Plunkett and a Meath man, but that in itself was enough to open the doors of the one and close the hearts of the other. In those days the native Irish and the Anglo-Irish formed two distinct and often opposed camps; the Confederation of Kilkenny had only papered over the differences and the collapse of the Confederation not only revealed them again but was in part caused by them. The Anglo-Irish, who were particularly strong in County Meath, had what seemed to the native Irish a divided loyalty. Descended from the Norman conquerors, they were almost all staunch Catholics and opponents of the Reformation; but at the same time, they were equally staunch supporters of the English King and of the English connection.

By his birth and breeding Oliver Plunkett belonged indisputably to the Anglo-Irish. He mixed on familiar terms with the gentry, he spoke English as fluently as he did Irish, he accepted without question that the English King was his lawful sovereign. The great majority of the clergy in Armagh diocese and in all the province apart from Meath were of the native Irish with native Irish names and attitudes; they spoke English with difficulty if they spoke it at all. They were drawn mainly from the peasantry, most of the Gaelic landowners having been dispossessed and driven into exile. Their allegiance to the English King was tenuous and shallow. To them a Meath man, any

Meath man, was someone to be viewed with suspicion.

It says a great deal for Oliver's tact and judgment that he should have won over so many of the clergy in so short a time. Barely six months after his arrival in Armagh, the Vicar-Generals of six of the northern dioceses wrote a joint letter to Rome thanking the Holy See for sending so illustrious a Primate to Ireland: "He is so untiring in good works and so exemplary in his life and conduct that he has won for himself and the clergy the love and reverence even of the enemies of our faith." They prefaced their remarks by saying that they had delayed writing until his merits were known to them by experience.

A minority of the clergy, however, both secular and religious, refused to be won over. During the Cromwellian period the Church as an organisation had vanished. The priests who remained operated on their own, dressed like the laity, lived with the laity, were subject to no superior. To many of them the arrival of a strong and reform-minded bishop was distinctly unwelcome. Oliver found great difficulty in trying to restore clerical discipline and he soon singled out drunkenness as one of the main obstacles to be overcome.

> While visiting six dioceses of this province, I made particular efforts to root out the cursed vice of drunkenness which is the parent and nurse of every scandal and dissension. I also decreed, under pain of deprivation of benefice, that no priest should frequent public houses,

drink whiskey, and so on. I myself have greatly profited from this decree and, as there is little use in preaching without practising, I no longer take a drink with my meals. Show me an Irish priest without this vice and he is surely a saint.

As Oliver began the systematic visitation of his province, he no doubt anticipated that he would have to deal with some clerical abuses. What he had not anticipated was *Praemunire*. "I must admit," he wrote later, "that when I first came to this kingdom I neither knew nor understood what was meant by the word *Praemunire*." He soon found that it was the Latin name for some old laws which made it an offence for anyone to exercise any authority derived from the Pope. This meant, for instance, that if a bishop were to remove a parish priest or discipline him in any way, he was guilty of *Praemunire* since his authority as a bishop came from the Pope. He could be taken to law by the parish priest, found guilty and imprisoned, while the priest continued undisturbed in his previous course of conduct.

Among the most notorious practitioners of this tactic was no less a dignitary than the Vicar-Apostolic of Derry, Terence O'Kelly. Despite his frequently scandalous way of life, all attempts to remove him had failed and he had got more than one of those sent against him imprisoned. Two previous Archbishops had trembled before him, but Oliver did not. He was a Plunkett and he knew that no court would bring in a verdict of guilty on such a trumped-up charge against a personal friend of the Governor of Ulster.

I went in person to the diocese of Derry, called the clergy together, suspended his jurisdiction, and appointed in his place Dr Conwell, a learned and holy man. I was charged before the civil court, but the unfortunate man found himself forestalled in the Vice-regal court, and in the court of the Governor of Ulster, the Earl of Charlemont. He thereupon cried out in a loud voice: "The Italian Primate, the Roman Primate, has unhorsed me!"

The Earl of Charlemont has not troubled even one ecclesiastic since I came here. He is so friendly with me that on one occasion, seeing me somewhat afraid, he said to me: "Have no fear, no-one shall dare touch you; and in future do not go to the mountains when you wish to administer confirmations, but come to the courtyard of my palace." He has made me a present during my lifetime of a garden and excellent orchard, with two fields and a fine house. It is in an excellent position.

As to the Viceroy, everyone knows that he has a high opinion of me and has even spoken to the King on my behalf. Dr Brennan, who has my cipher, will tell you more about this. I will only mention here that at my request he reprieved three Catholics who had been tried and sentenced to death in the city of Enniskillen.

The Earl of Drogheda allows me to have a public church with bells, etc., in that part of my diocese which lies inside his territory, which is exempt from royal jurisdiction.

I have been accused before the Viceroy on no fewer than nine occasions in connection with the schools and for having exercised foreign jurisdiction. This nobleman, however, always had these charges brought to his own court and thus they were quashed.

The Viceroy referred to, Lord Berkeley, had been appointed to Dublin in May, 1670, two months after Oliver's arrival in Ireland. He got on well with Oliver from the beginning and was a welcome change from his predecessor, the bigoted and intolerant Roberts. During his first two months or so in Ireland, Oliver did not dare appear openly in public but he did not let this unduly restrict his activities. He travelled around under the disguise of an army captain, an unlikely disguise for the scholarly archbishop but perhaps all the more effective for that.

Imagination has to work hard to envisage Oliver in the role of the swashbuckling Captain Brown, a part one would have thought more suited to the talents of an Errol Flynn: clattering into the courtyard of the little country inn, dismounting with a jangle of sword and spurs, quaffing a tankard, singing a song, stealing the customary kiss from the customary buxom serving-wench, then disappearing down the road again in a swirl of dust and hoofbeats. To us these are the tired clichés of the romantic cinema: to Oliver they were, as we shall see, for many weeks a daily reality.

The departure of Roberts meant also the departure of Captain Brown. With the well-disposed Berkeley now ruling Ireland in the King's name, Oliver could go freely about his work. It is a mistake to imagine that he spent all his time in Ireland as a hunted man. There were plenty of anti-Catholic laws on the statute-books but they were not enforced in any systematic way. It was illegal to open a Catholic church or school, but a powerful local magnate like the Earl of Drogheda could ignore the law. It was *Praemunire* for a bishop to exercise his jurisdiction but a sympathetic magistrate could dismiss the charge or impose a nominal penalty. It all depended on the political climate of the day and much of Oliver's efforts went towards bringing about a suitable climate for the work of the Church and doing as much as possible while it lasted. It is not surprising, in view of his past experiences, that he expressed this in a nautical metaphor.

This is the time for doing good work, while the present Viceroy is with us. We must follow the example of sailors at sea. When the wind is favourable, they unfurl all their canvas and skim swiftly across the ocean under full sail; but when it turns against them, they lower their sails and take shelter in some little port. While we have the present Viceroy, we may sail; and I will do all in my power to advance our spiritual interests, instruct the clergy, and educate them in science and theology.

## 4. A MAN IN A HURRY

The first four years of Oliver's primacy, 1670, 1671, 1672 and 1673, were years when the sun shone and the winds blew favourably. Knowing that the weather could change at any moment, Oliver crowded on every possible inch of canvas. He never knew when there might be a change of Viceroys or a change of law or a change of policy and this spurred him to extraordinary activity. Like any man in a hurry, he made occasional mistakes, stepped on occasional toes, made occasional enemies. Still, the record of his achievements during his first six months makes astonishing reading as set out in the letter of the northern Vicar-Generals referred to above.

> Since he arrived in the province of Armagh, he has never stopped working. He called together diocesan synods which were of great benefit to the province, he instructed the clergy by word and example, and in the ordinations which he held he ordained only those who were fully worthy and had passed a strict examination.
>
> He held a provincial council in the town of

Clones in which many useful decrees were passed; and to the great joy of the clergy and of all Catholics, he suspended the jurisdiction of Terence O'Kelly, Vicar of Derry, a thing which many others had previously attempted to do without success.

He brought the Fathers of the Society of Jesus into the diocese of Armagh to educate the youth and give instruction to the younger priests, and he built a house and schools for them at his own expense.

In the dioceses of Armagh, Kilmore, Clogher, Derry, Down, Connor and Dromore, in spite of the huge distances involved, he administered confirmation to thousands in the woods and mountains, regardless of winds and rain.

Furthermore, he recently achieved a work which will greatly benefit the whole Catholic community. There were many men of noble family who had lost all their property and been publicly declared outlaws, and who had subsequently been responsible for many crimes of violence. He persuaded them to change their way of life for the better and got them a pardon for their crimes; and not only a pardon for themselves but for all those who sheltered or supported them. In this way hundreds and hundreds of Catholic families have been rescued from great danger to their bodies, souls and properties.

Of the various good works listed, the last-named was the most controversial. A number of dispossessed Catholics had taken to the hills where they led a kind of guerrilla existence and lived by robbing and blackmailing the people of the area around the borders of Armagh and Tyrone. They were known as Tories or Rapparees and at first enjoyed a certain glamour as freedom fighters against the English intruders. But by 1670 the glamour had worn off and the local people had become thoroughly disillusioned with their self-appointed protectors. If they supported the Rapparees, they were harassed and fined by the government; if they did not, they were liable to be robbed and even murdered by the Rapparees themselves.

Oliver undertook to act as intermediary between the Rapparees and the government. At considerable danger to himself, he met them on the border of County Tyrone and spent an hour talking to them about the dangers to the body and soul which they were bringing upon themselves and their fellow-Catholics. He found the unfortunate men at the end of their tether and willing to grasp at any way out of their predicament. Eventually he succeeded in securing pardons for them and for two of their comrades who were in prison under sentence of death, under condition that they left the country.

The role of the peacemaker is often an ungrateful one. Though the ordinary people of the locality were deeply thankful for the deliverance, he found himself under attack from other sources. The Secretary of Propaganda in Rome, who considered that negotiating with bandits was conduct unbecoming an Archbishop, wrote him a sharp letter of rebuke. Those Rapparees who remained on in various parts of the province denounced him violently as a willing tool of the English in their work of subjugating the Irish. Unkindest cut of all, he was accused at his trial of having been in league with the Rapparees all the time against the English government and of having got them out of the country so that they could organise an army in France for the invasion of Ireland.

The duty of administering the sacrament of confirmation was a less dangerous but much more laborious one. Most of the dioceses of Ireland had not had a resident bishop for twenty years and as a result many people, adults as well as children, had never been confirmed. It was Oliver's custom during his visitation of his province to administer the sacrament to the people of each district and to keep careful record of the numbers involved. Since there were few Catholic churches in the country and most of them very small, the confirmation ceremony was usually held in the open air. The Earl of Charlemont, as we have seen, offered the use of his courtyard for this purpose; but in other places, where the local grandee was less helpful or the spies more dangerous, some out-of-the-way wood or mountain valley had to be used.

It is a pity that Oliver has not given us a full description of one of these scenes; probably he had become so accustomed to them that he took the strange surroundings for granted. By the end of 1670 he had covered most of the main centres of population and during 1671 he continued on into the remoter areas, including the mountains of Donegal. When a new Vicar-General was appointed for Raphoe (Donegal), it was Oliver himself who led him through the mountain passes of this not very prepossessing area. In a letter written to Rome soon afterwards, the Vicar-General described his feelings.

> It is for spiritual motives alone that I have taken on the responsibility for so barren, rough and rugged a place. I admit too that I was moved by the words and even more by the example of the illustrious Primate; for he has on many occasions administered confirmation to the children in these very mountains and woods. On many occasions too he has had nothing to eat but oaten bread, salty butter and stirabout, and nothing to drink but milk.
>
> We are all amazed that a man of such a delicate constitution, who was accustomed (as I myself know) to so many amenities in Rome, should be able to undergo so many labours, so many journeys, so much hardship and adversities. It is quite certain that if he does not change his way of living and acting, he will lose his health and become useless to himself and to others.

It is the first mention we have of Oliver's health; it will not be the last.

Among the many factors that depressed the new Vicar-General of Raphoe, the state of the clergy ranked high. "The labourers are few," he wrote, "and they have little knowledge of the art of arts, that is, the guidance of souls. There are about fourteen priests, of whom only one has ever been

outside this country; and he, although he studied
in Louvain, is not altogether right in the head. His
name is Louis Gallagher. The others had a super-
ficial training in grammar and poetry and some
cases of conscience, according to the local
custom."

Oliver himself had become aware of the same
problem at an early stage in his journeys and the
question of schools soon became one of his chief
concerns. Catholics had now been without schools
for twenty years and the lack of education was
becoming very apparent among the younger priests
and the whole Catholic community. It was obviously impossible for Oliver to provide education
on any wide scale but even one well-run school
could help to educate an elite, the future clerical
and lay leaders of the Catholic community. He set
about starting such a school with his customary
dispatch, choosing a site in Drogheda where he
enjoyed the protection of the Earl and securing the
services of two priests of the Society of Jesus,
which enjoyed a very high reputation in the field
of education. In April 1671 he wrote to Rome to
report on progress and ask for financial aid:

> The nobility and gentry of the whole province
> of Ulster, with only three exceptions, have lost
> all their lands and from being owners have
> become tenants; they now have no means to
> educate their children. The young priests who
> were ordained during the past seven years to fill
> the place of those who had died have very little
> education as they had no-one qualified to teach
> them; in fact, Catholic teachers were not

tolerated at all.

I undertook to deal with the problem. I invited the Jesuit fathers to my diocese; I built a good-sized house for them from the ground up, together with two schools where about 150 boys and 25 clerics are being educated; and for the past nine months I have supported two very learned and hard-working Jesuits, with one lay-brother and one servant.

One of the fathers spends an hour every morning and afternoon giving the clerics instruction in cases of morality and in methods of preaching and teaching catechism; he also teaches the lay pupils for two hours in the morning and another two hours in the evening. On feast days and holidays he teaches the ceremonies and the manner of administering the sacraments, etc. The other Jesuit is occupied in teaching syntax and grammar, etc. In addition, both of them are engaged in preaching. I have supported them for the past nine months and have bought them everything down to the smallest piece of furniture.

Propaganda no doubt had its own problems, and it was not until September of the following year that Oliver received news that money was to be sent for the support of the Jesuits. He wrote at once to express his gratitude and to describe the progress of the school with understandable pride.

I have just received your most welcome letter of the 2nd of September and this whole kingdom is indebted to you for providing the Jesuits with a stipend. They are doing very good work and now have in Drogheda, in my diocese, 160 students. But I had to go through such troubles and make such efforts to support them; and there were so many protests sent to the Viceroy and the Supreme Council against me and against them.

They gave all the more offence to our ill-wishers because they are in Drogheda, which is only four hours' journey from Dublin where no Catholic schools are allowed; and to have there the Jesuits, whom they hate more than any others, was to add insult to injury.

Yet now these very same ill-wishers are paying court both to me and to them in order to get their children into the schools; and in fact they now have many Protestant boys from the leading families who come to our defence.

Monsignor, I solemnly assure you that I spent more than 400 scudi [£100] on them during the past two years and two months and we are still in debt for 200 scudi. I dressed in cloth of a half-scudo a yard, I kept only one servant and a boy to look after my horses, and I cut down on my food, in order to help the Jesuits. The Viceroy gave me a half promise that he would not disturb them; but when the money promised by the King did not arrive, I must admit I found it very difficult to keep them going and became very depressed in spirits. Now, however, your letter brings me great joy.

It would appear that some at least of the clerics referred to were not students but young priests who came to Drogheda to learn after ordination what they were unable to learn before; in 1673

Oliver refers to fifty young priests as having benefited from the Jesuit teachers, who by this time numbered three. He rightly felt that raising the standard of the clergy was one of the best services he could give the Irish Church. What Ireland needed was not more priests but better priests; indeed, from the point of view of mere quantity, the country had too many. In August of the same year he wrote:

> There are too many secular priests here. Every gentleman wants to have his own chaplain and to have Mass said under his own roof, under pretext of being afraid of the Government. They force the bishops to ordain priests and afterwards they move heaven and earth to obtain a parish for this priest, their dependent. The remedy for this would be to withdraw from me and from all the archbishops and bishops of this kingdom permission to ordain outside the specified times.

The letter goes on to ask for six places in the Irish College for students from three of the northern dioceses. This was a favourite theme of Oliver's. Though conscious of how much the Drogheda schools were doing, he was equally conscious of how much they lacked, especially when compared with the great universities of Rome. He had in an earlier letter already made a request for six places for students in the Propaganda College and given his reasons at length: only a Roman education could fit a priest to occupy a position of leadership in the Church.

Those educated in Rome are better acquainted with the wishes of the Holy See, they know its thinking, they are better able to communicate with it. The Piazza di Spagna, the Propaganda, indeed the whole of Rome, are one great book. There are so many nationalities to be seen there, each with its own customs. Poles, Germans, Spaniards, French, Indians, Turks, Ethiopians, Africans, Americans can be met there; and one learns what skill and judgment are needed to reconcile the various opinions and opposing interests of so many different nationalities.

The changes in the government have also a lesson to teach. One observes the modest and wise and humble behaviour of those who the previous day or under the previous Pope were all-powerful and honoured by everyone: they keep faith equally in prosperity and adversity. I was especially impressed by the prelates Cajetan and Massimi, and another from Modena who had been Governor of Rome in the time of Alexander VII of happy memory, and many others in the time of Innocent and Urban. One comes into contact with cardinals and prelates of great wisdom and prudence, learned and experienced in spiritual affairs and in the temporal affairs of so many rulers and princes. It is impossible for anyone of reasonable ability not to advance greatly in knowledge and experience.

And indeed to educate a missionary priest, there is no college in the world better suited than the Propaganda, where the students are instructed for two hours every morning in theology, and after dinner for an hour in controversy, and later for half an hour or an hour in cases of conscience. They learn to preach and to master Hebrew and Greek; they take part in the Church ceremonies and are trained in Gregorian chant; they receive in short an education which is better fitted for missionaries than that of any other college.

Therefore I anxiously implore that I may be allowed to send half a dozen of the most talented young priests that I can find to be educated in that college so that my unfortunate province of Ulster may have men able to govern its churches; for if God were to take from us in Ulster three men, Thomas Fitzsimons, Dr Conwell and Dr Ronan Maginn, there would be no-one else with the necessary learning or skill to govern these churches. The other Vicar-Generals are of no more than average ability.

If you do not grant me this favour, we shall be without leaders, without shepherds, and the wolves will devour our flocks. The Roman—that is, the man educated in Rome—has the knowledge and the ability to govern. The prince of poets has fittingly sung:

*Tu regere imperio populos, Romane, memento:*
*Hae tibi erunt artes. . . .*


This is one of the most touching and revealing of Oliver's letters to Rome. There was no need for him to describe the City and its sights to the Secretaries of a Roman Congregation; he was writing not for them but for himself. The memories began to flood out as he wrote and his pen could hardly keep pace with them. The newly-arrived youth in the Piazza di Spagna, gazing at the passing crowds, seeing perhaps a black man for the first time in his life. The student in the university corridor arguing in fractured Latin and Italian with Poles and Germans and Italians and French. The young priest at the beginning of his career observing how yesterday's dispensers of patronage became today's forgotten men. The professor in Propaganda preparing his lectures in theology and controversy for the eager young missionaries-to-be. The maturing scholar who finds the perfect quotation from Virgil rising unbidden to his lips: "Be mindful, Roman, of thy destiny to rule the peoples with thy sceptre: these shall be thy arts."

As he sent the letter on its way from his bleak and barbarous nation, a little of his heart went with it.

One would like to know, though, what kind of Americans were to be seen in Rome in the middle of the seventeenth century.

## 5. UNFINISHED BUSINESS

At the beginning of 1671, with a good deal of his province already visited, Oliver began to make plans for a journey to the islands of Scotland. He had been asked by Propaganda to look after the spiritual needs of the Catholics living in the Hebrides, who spoke a form of Gaelic similar to Ulster Irish, and to appoint some Irish priests to minister there. Oliver found his plans running into difficulties with the Marquis of Antrim, an Irish Catholic nobleman who had succeeded in recovering his estates and was a power in Antrim and the isles. Oliver's letter on the subject showed that he retained both his Roman memories and his sense of humour.

The visitation of the Hebrides still remains to be done; but if the Sacred Congregation does not write a letter to the Marquis of Antrim, we shall not be able to accomplish anything. This nobleman has great influence in the islands but he has many traits in common with Monsignor Alberici, good and prudent, but slow and cautious about everything. I remember that Monsignor Alberici could not find a servant to suit him in the whole of Italy. From Florence, they were talkative; from Milan, they were giddy; from the Romagna, they were stupid; from Naples, they were light-fingered; from Rome, they were too gloomy.

It is equally difficult to find anyone to please the Marquis of Antrim. I suggested at least twenty priests to him but he had some objection to every one of them; and about Ronan Maginn, a very suitable man for the task, he remarked that he seemed to be over-hasty and presumptuous and proud. The chief cause of the delay is the treaty of union between Scotland and England, as I mentioned in a previous letter.

The Marquis sent three priests to the islands to administer the sacraments of Penance and the Eucharist during Lent. After Easter they came back, unwilling to stay there all the year round as they had good parishes in County Antrim. Anyhow, they are very old and not able for the hard work of the islands.

A courteous letter to this nobleman, praising his piety and his zeal for the spiritual good of these souls, would be of great help in this affair. I spent three days with him at his home in Dunluce. It is a splendid building. The palace is perched upon a high rock, lashed on every side by the sea. It is only twelve miles distant from the largest of the Hebrides.

Monsignor, this letter is essential, as the Marquis is the only Catholic nobleman who can help me in this mission. Without his assistance I would run many risks.

In June of the same year, he wrote again to ask

for money to help with the expenses of his journey to the Hebrides.

> I need some assistance to enable me to visit the Scottish islands, that is, the Hebrides. Without your assistance I can do nothing. I shall have to bring a priest and a servant with me and to dress in the kind of clothes worn by the local people, which are different from those worn anywhere else in the world.

The picture of the Archbishop of Armagh dressing himself in kilt and bonnet at the expense of the Vatican is a pleasing one. But it would appear that the projected visit never took place. One reason was the continuing lack of money: in September he informed Propaganda that "the spirit is willing but the cash is weak." More important were the political complications referred to in his earlier letter. The visit of an Irish archbishop might be taken as an attempt to stir up the Catholic islanders against the proposed union with England and so bring fresh persecution upon their heads. So Oliver was forced to continue looking after the island people from a distance.

At home there were plenty of other matters to engage his attention. He could not bear the thought of unfinished business. He continued his travels tirelessly and sent a stream of detailed reports to Rome on every place he visited and everyone he met. He sent lists of the names of all the secular priests in the northern dioceses with a short character sketch of each. Most of them were men of blameless lives but occasional exceptions were noted: "given somewhat to drink", "weak in doctrine", "frequents taverns and is under suspicion regarding observance of chastity but has promised reform", "fathered children as a young man; sent concubine away but is somewhat addicted to drink."

There were irregularities too among the regular clergy, that is, the religious orders. Of these the Franciscans were by far the most numerous and, by the law of averages, it was only to be expected that most of his troubles with religious involved Franciscans. The friars had shown great heroism during the time of Cromwell and had stuck to their posts through thick and thin; for this they were held in universal respect by the people. But the hard times had taken their toll and discipline had grown lax in some of the smaller communities.

Oliver's attempts at reform were hampered not only by the normal stubbornness of human nature but by the fact that the Franciscans were to a large extent exempt from the authority of the local bishop. He asked without much success for additional powers to deal with them. He complained that they had too many small, badly run novitiates. He complained that Irish Franciscan communities on the continent used Ireland as a dumping place for misfits and malcontents. He complained about the friars questing, that is, asking alms, in parish churches on Sunday; sometimes Mass was held up for hours while friars and farmers haggled over pigs and geese and vegetables. The friars also complained about the meddlesome archbishop and accused him of everything from simony to judicial murder. So tense was the situation that Oliver believed his life to be in danger from one of the friars, Anthony Daly of Armagh. Writing in January 1680 he described a frightening experience of six years earlier.

> This Father Anthony made an attempt on my life and instigated the Tories to kill me. They came to the house of my Vicar-general, where I was then staying, around midnight. They burst open the doors and took away all the money from myself and my vicar-general and my secretary, Michael Plunkett, who is now in Rome, and they held a sword to my throat.
>
> The leader of this band was arrested afterwards. In prison, before his death, he declared to the parish priest of Armagh and to his curate that Fr Anthony had told him to kill me and said that he would give him absolution afterwards.

It would be tedious to go into the innumerable ramifications of the innumerable disputes involving the Archbishop and the clergy. It will be sufficient to recount one of the best-known of these, his intervention in the quarrel between the Franciscans and the Dominicans over the ownership of three friaries. He intervened with some reluctance: "If I decide in favour of the Dominicans, the whole body of the Franciscans will write and publish a thousand accusations and a thousand calumnies against me, saying that this primate is an enemy of the Franciscans, and so on. And vice versa if I decide in favour of the Franciscans." On instructions from Rome, however, he investigated the affair and after a long and careful inquiry judged in favour of the Dominicans.

His lengthy report on the subject is worth reading in full. It shows his ordered mind at its best, calm, judicial, impartial, cutting away inessentials and marshalling the essential facts in clear and logical order.

> I examined the controversy between the Dominicans and Franciscans of the province of Armagh by the authority delegated from Rome as well as by my ordinary authority. I found the arguments put forward by the Dominicans to be the stronger and gave judgment in their favour. The Franciscans however have appealed to the Holy See from my decision and sent a special agent to Rome to present their appeal. Therefore I think it necessary to send Your Excellency an account of the whole matter in as short a space as possible.
>
> The Dominican Fathers of this province have three friaries about which there is no controversy: that is, the friaries of Drogheda, Derry, and Bannina or Coleraine. There is no dispute about these. All the controversy is about three other friaries, namely, Newtown in the diocese of Down, Gaula in Clogher, and Carlingford in my own diocese.
>
> I went to the County Down, called together the parties to the dispute, and found the clearest evidence that the friary of Newtown belonged to the Dominicans. St Antoninus makes mention of it in the third part of his history; and Sir James

Ware in his book *De Antiquitatibus Hiberniae* says on page 212 about the friary of Down: "The friary of the Order of Preachers was founded in 1244 and chapters of the order were held there in 1298 and 1312; it is situated in the territory of Ards near the sea-shore." Moreover, witnesses were produced who swore that they had seen Dominicans of this friary questing in the diocese of Down before the time of Cromwell.

In the diocese of Armagh I summoned before me the parties to the dispute about the friary of Carlingford. The Dominicans again invoked the authority of Ware, who writes on page 203: "In Carlingford a friary of the Order of Preachers under the patronage of the Earls of Ulster." They also produced a document of the tenth year of Henry VIII by which a citizen of Carlingford named Mariman made over a house and garden to the Dominicans of the friary of Carlingford. Again, in the Dublin Register called *Defective Titles* there is a mention of this friary of the Dominicans at Carlingford. They also brought forward the evidence of old people who had seen some Dominican friars living near this friary before the war of Cromwell.

I went to the diocese of Clogher and summoned the contending parties to the Franciscan Friary near Enniskillen. The Dominicans adduced the authority of the ancient annals of that town, written in the Irish language, which give the name of the friary of Gaula, the year in which it was founded, and the name of the Pope under whom it was founded for the Dominicans. They brought forward in addition an old priest who swore that he heard from his father that the friary of Gaula belonged to the Dominicans. They also produced other witnesses who gave similar evidence.

The Franciscans, on the other hand, could bring forward nothing but negative evidence. They produced the signatures of people who testified that they had never seen or heard of the Dominicans being in these friaries. They claimed that the people were not able to support both Dominicans and Franciscans. They said that the secular clergy were opposed to the Dominicans. They went around collecting the signatures of the gentry and others against the Dominicans and they went so far as to approach Protestant gentlemen and ask them to speak to me against the Dominicans. Many of these did in fact speak to me and virtually threatened me if I did not remove the Dominicans from these dioceses.

The Franciscans argued finally that the Dominicans, even if they once owned these friaries, had lost all right to them as they had abandoned and deserted them for many years, so that prescription now held against them. The Dominicans however replied that in time of war, pestilence and persecution, no prescription holds good against those who abandon their friaries.

These were in essence the principal arguments on either side which, with the whole of the proceedings, I submitted to the Bishop of Meath, to Dr Thomas Fitzsimons, Vicar-General of Kilmore, and to Dr Oliver Dease, Vicar-General of Meath. They were of the opinion that I should decide in favour of the Dominicans and I did so.

Here it must be remarked that the Dominicans came to live in these dioceses near these friaries upon the restoration of the King and the ending of Cromwell's persecution, that is, seven or eight years before I came to this country; so I did not introduce them here but found them already in possession.

Considering, then, the arguments brought forward by the Dominicans and considering that I found them already in possession of their residences in these dioceses; considering too the great good that they do, having able preachers and learned men among them; finally, considering that both orders have sufficient for their support in these dioceses since they supported themselves here for the last ten years in spite of their disputes, and could support themselves far better if they lived at peace, since many people are so scandalised at their quarrels that they will give alms to neither; in consideration of all these things I deemed myself bound in conscience to give judgment in favour of the Dominicans.

On publication of the verdict, the Franciscans appealed to the Holy See and it seemed as if all Hell broke loose upon me. Among the accusations, it was said that I gave judgment without listening to both sides; yet the Very Reverend Paul O'Neill, who goes as their representative to Rome, was present when I heard both sides in the diocese of Dromore, as were also Dr Ronan Maginn, Vicar-Apostolic of Dromore, and twenty other priests and friars. In the diocese of Clogher, the inquiry was held in the friary of the Franciscans themselves; and while I was holding this session I got a severe attack of illness.

As to my own diocese, everyone knows that I heard them. The crowd that assembled was so large, even though some miles distant from the city, that it requires downright barefacedness to say that I did not examine the matter. Still, they threaten me time and again that they will treat me as they treated my predecessor, Richard of Armagh, who was summoned to Avignon and died there of grief. The guardian of Dundalk told me this to my face.

It is unnecessary for me to say any more as Your Excellency is both wise enough and concerned enough to settle the matter properly. I would ask you to show this letter, as also all my other letters, to Dr Peter Creagh, our agent in Rome, to keep him informed of the affairs of the province, and I shall ever remain,

Your most obliged and obedient servant,

Oliver of Armagh,
*Dundalk, 8th September, 1672.*

The violent reaction of the Franciscans in Ireland was re-echoed abroad. In the library of St Isidore's, the Irish Franciscan House in Rome, a bust of the Archbishop had recently been set up. Two of the students, John McMoyer and Hugh Duffy, demonstrated their feelings on the subject by knocking the head off the bust. For this they were expelled but afterwards gained admission to the Franciscan novitiate in Spain and eventually returned to Ireland. Nine years later they were to have their revenge.

One other point worth mentioning in the letter is the reference to Oliver's illness. We are given no clue as to its nature and he refers to it not for its own sake but to refute the suggestion that he had not held a proper inquiry; obviously his illness during the inquiry had been a talking-point and had fixed the event in everyone's mind. There can be little doubt, however, that the Archbishop's health was beginning to deteriorate under the constant strain to which he was subjected.

## 6. THE TWO PRIMATES

There was one ecclesiastical controversy which had a rather special character in that it involved Oliver not with the lower clergy but with an equal, or at least one who claimed to be an equal. This was Peter Talbot, Archbishop of Dublin, who had initially welcomed the appointment of the new Archbishop of Armagh but had since come to revise his opinion.

The work of re-establishing the hierarchy begun in 1669 had been taken a step further in 1671 with the appointment of another six bishops. Among them was Oliver's old friend, John Brennan, whom he had left behind in Rome and who now returned to Ireland as Bishop of Waterford. The country now had a hierarchy of four archbishops and eight bishops; and at the head of that hierarchy, by immemorial custom, was the Archbishop of Armagh in his capacity of Primate of All Ireland.

That was Oliver Plunkett's view of the situation, a view not shared by Peter Talbot.

Talbot was a colourful cleric, even in that age of colourful clerics. He came from an Anglo-Irish family every bit as distinguished as Oliver's but his career had followed very different lines. An ardent royalist, he had joined the Jesuits and during the period when Cromwell ruled England he had attached himself to the exiled Charles II. All governments in exile live by plot and counter-plot; intrigue is their life-blood, rumour is the air they breathe. Talbot loved every minute of it and was constantly engaged in cloak-and-dagger missions for his royal master, all of them unfathomably mysterious but of the highest importance. One would be tempted to describe him as the typical Jesuit of fiction but for the fact that he found his membership of the Society hampering his work and resigned to join the secular clergy. Charles did not forget his faithful henchman when restored to the English throne and it was partly at his urging that Talbot was appointed to the See of Dublin in 1669.

The first clash between the two archbishops occurred at the Synod held in Dublin in June, 1670. Reviving a half-forgotten historical claim, Talbot sought to preside at the Synod on the grounds that the Archbishop of Dublin was Primate of Ireland. Oliver contested this claim on the grounds that his bull of appointment gave him the title of Primate while Talbot's did not. Talbot further complicated the issue by claiming to have a document from the King appointing him head of the Irish hierarchy in civil affairs, but was either unable or unwilling to produce it. It was finally agreed to let Oliver preside and refer the matter to Rome for a decision.

There matters should have rested but did not.

Throughout 1671 the dispute about the primacy
simmered on. The followers of the two archbishops continued to argue the case, with the
inevitable result of driving the principals further
apart. Both wrote to Rome complaining about the
activities of the other. Oliver was worried that
Talbot's continuing political intrigues were threatening the peace of the Church in Ireland; he had
already antagonised the tolerant Viceroy, Berkeley,
and was in danger of being exiled. In March 1671
Oliver wrote:

> The Viceroy, who in any event has little love
> for Dr Talbot and his family, had for these and
> other reasons made up his mind to banish him
> from the kingdom. I did everything in my power
> to dissuade the Viceroy and humbly begged him
> not to take this course of action. At the same
> time, I assured him that whatever difference
> there might be between the Archbishop of
> Dublin and myself over the question of juris-
> diction, we were still friends. His Excellency was
> appeased and said he was edified by my inter-
> vention on behalf of Dr Talbot.

Talbot and his supporters were by no means
behind-hand in making counter-accusations against
the Archbishop of Armagh. They told Rome that
he was imprudent and autocratic, that he had acted
rashly in setting up schools and becoming involved
with the Tories, that he was over-friendly with the
Protestants and particularly with the Duke of
Ormond (an old enemy of the Talbot family). All
this was routine stuff; but Roman eyebrows must

have been raised when the further accusation was made that Dr Plunkett's relations with women were causing scandal and that he had been guilty of sexual misconduct on a number of occasions.

This was too much. Oliver wrote indignantly to answer the charges; but his answer must have caused even more astonishment in Rome than the original accusations:

> I said some time ago that if I published the decree in favour of the Dominicans there would be no end to the slanders made against me. I assure Your Excellency that since the present Viceroy came to this kingdom (that is, during the past two years), no living being can accuse me of having done anything unbecoming my sacred office. I ask you to note this statement carefully. Yes; distinguish the times and you shall reconcile the scriptures.
>
> During the time of the previous Viceroy, Roberts, who pursued me with great hostility, I was forced to conceal myself by going around under the name of Captain Brown, with a sword and wig and pistols and so on; this lasted for two or three months. When I visited a house or went into a tavern, I used to kiss the women, I used to sing, and on one occasion when some non-Catholics with me seemed suspicious of my identity, I took up on my horse with me the wife of the gentleman in whose house I was then staying and we rode together for a mile accompanied by the lady's brother, who was a Catholic. All this took place two years ago. I ask you therefore to read these accusations carefully and to be on your guard if the writer speaks in

general terms.

One would dearly love to know how this letter was received in the Sacred Congregation for the Propagation of the Faith. Discreet archiepiscopal amours they had encountered before, but this kind of behaviour was totally outside their experience. It seemed to have all the disadvantages of a public scandal without any of the private compensations. What exchanging was there of remarks and glances, what helpless shrugging of soft monsignorial shoulders, what raising of brown Italian eyes to Heaven? Or had they by now reached the stage where nothing they read in any letter from Ireland could surprise them any more?

Almost simultaneously with the arrival of this letter in Rome in the late spring of 1672 came others from Ireland reporting on the latest exploit of the unpredictable Primate. A book had just appeared in Dublin, entitled *Jus Primatiale or The Ancient Right and Preheminency of the See of Armagh above all Archbishopricks in the Kingdom of Ireland*. The author's name was veiled under the initials O.A.T.H.P. but it required no great power of divination to interpret this as *Oliverius Armacanus Totius Hiberniae Primas,*that is, Oliver of Armagh, Primate of All Ireland.

This short work has a special interest as the only formal piece of literature written by Oliver. It is a slim, small volume, the pages measuring just over six inches by four. It is written in English, but with plentiful quotations from Latin documents, and it opens with a five-page introduction in which the writer declares his aim of rescuing Armagh's primacy "from the Worm of Oblivion, which often proveth to be the Mother of Ignorance".

There are 75 pages in the main body of the book and a 76th is devoted to correcting errata. The opening pages may be quoted in full as they show once again Oliver's knack of getting straight to the essence of his subject and of answering the reader's questions before he has time to ask them. The spelling and punctuation have been brought into line with modern usage; otherwise it is as Oliver wrote it.

The first occasion of the difference between the Archbishop of Armagh and the Archbishop of Dublin concerning precedency and other points of superiority and jurisdiction happened in a meeting of all the archbishops and bishops of the Roman Catholic profession in the month of June, 1670, in Dublin, when they were subscribing a remonstrance of their loyalty to be presented to his Excellency the Lord Berkeley, each of them refusing to subscribe subsequently to the other; which contestation did displease many, both in this Kingdom and in foreign countries, for the three ensuing reasons.

*First,* they are and were in a country governed and for the most part inhabited by those of a contrary profession.

*Secondly,* prelates of the Church in giving honour ought to go one before the other, not in seeking honour.*

---

* The meaning of this is that prelates of the Church ought to outdo one another in giving honour, not in seeking it.

*Thirdly*, that archbishops and bishops should increase their reputation by modesty and not by ambition.

I confess these to be good and sound reasons and ought to move the ecclesiastical superiors to all modesty and humility, consistent with the honour and jurisdiction of the prelacy they exercise; but to prejudice the dignity of the See committed to their charge and also their successors would render them odious to all posterity, and argue breach of trust and weakness in them; and therefore, from the very time of the Apostles to this day, both ecclesiastical and secular superiors strived to maintain the right of the dignities and offices imposed on them.

The author then cites a number of instances of eminent clerics engaging in disputes about precedence, before passing on to the main argument. An impressive array of authorities is quoted, including the ancient life of St Patrick by Jocelinus and a bull of Pope Urban IV in 1263. Talbot himself is referred to only indirectly, and then more in sorrow than in anger: "It is a doleful thing that passion should alter the judgments of great men, as Aristotle saith in his Rhetorics." The work ends with the pious hope that attempts to challenge the primacy of Armagh "shall have no effect for the future to prejudice the pre-eminence of that ancient and most illustrious See in its superiority over all other archbishoprics in this Kingdom of Ireland."

There is no doubt that Oliver believed he was in the right not only in defending the primacy of

Armagh but in defending it at that time and in that way. He was conscious of the arguments in favour of silence and had consciously rejected them. The primacy of his See had been maintained for more than a thousand years and it was his clear and bounden duty to continue to maintain it. He would not shirk that duty, no matter what pain or scandal he might cause others by so doing.

The pained and the scandalised naturally included the Archbishop of Dublin, who wrote at once to complain of Oliver's "imprudence and inconsistency". More significantly, they included one reasonably impartial observer, Dr John Brennan, the newly arrived Bishop of Waterford. Despite his old friendship with Oliver, he did not conceal his dismay at the course events were taking. He sent Rome an account of what he called a "noisy and scandalous dispute".

> While I was in Dublin I tried discreetly but persistently to reconcile them, and I tried to do the same by writing from here. All I succeeded in getting was fair promises and a superficial patching-up of differences. I will keep on doing everything in my power but without much hope since both of them are hot-tempered and the dispute has now become public in England as well as in Ireland. As a result, most of the Catholics are divided in favour of one or the other. I have also been told by an important person that in Dublin the Protestant ministers are talking with great delight about this controversy, even from the pulpits.

In a letter to the Internuncio in Brussels a few days later, Brennan used similar terms about the two disputants: "they are both of them touchy and hot-tempered". Of all the countless accusations made against Oliver to the Roman Curia, this is the only one that strikes home. It was made not by an enemy but by a friend of twenty-five years' standing and it was made not once but twice in the measured language of official reports. If John Brennan described him as touchy and hot-tempered then we can safely take it that he was touchy and hot-tempered.

In November of that year Oliver wrote to the Internuncio to report that he and Talbot had settled their differences.

> Through the efforts of the Bishop of Killaloe, perfect harmony has been restored between the Archbishop of Dublin and myself. Dr Talbot, his brothers and nephews, and I, all had dinner together; and in the evening Dr Talbot and his brothers came to visit all my friends, something that has not happened this past twelve months. We shall send all documents relating to the controversy to Rome and shall await a decision in peace and tranquillity.

John Brennan was less optimistic. "The Archbishops of Armagh and Dublin have been getting along smoothly since their reconciliation," he wrote in January 1673, "but I doubt if it will last very long." His prophecy was never tested. Before the end of the year, Talbot was to be in exile, Plunkett and Brennan in hiding, and the dispute about the primacy thrust back into the obscurity from which it should never have emerged.

## 7. FLIGHT IN WINTER

In August 1672 the friendly Viceroy Berkeley (whose wife, Oliver discovered, was a Catholic) had been replaced by the Earl of Essex. Essex was a complex man, conscientious but irresolute; he was prepared to continue Berkeley's policy of toleration as long as he was free from outside pressures. But Ireland could never be long unaffected by events in the neighbouring island and the year 1673 was marked by an outburst of anti-Catholic feeling in England which pitted an increasingly Protestant Parliament against an increasingly Catholic court. The revelation that the Duke of York, the King's brother and heir to the throne, had been for years a secret Catholic caused a storm in Parliament. The Duke was forced to resign from his post of Lord High Admiral and the King promised a stricter enforcement of the laws against Popery.

Essex had no choice but to follow the lead of his royal master. On October 27 an edict was issued which closed all Catholic schools and religious houses and banished all Ordinaries (that is, bishops and vicar-generals) and all regular clergy from the country. They were ordered to register at one of the designated sea-ports and wait there until a vessel was ready to take them to exile on the Continent.

The simple thing to do was to register and then hope that the normal inertia of Irish administration would prevent any further action being taken. The ageing Patrick Plunkett, Bishop of Meath, gave in his name at Dublin, as did the Bishop of Killaloe; the Archbishop of Tuam registered in Galway, and others elsewhere.

Oliver decided not to register. It was his first clear and open flouting of the law. Up to this he had been operating in the shadowy area between legality and illegality, relying on personal contacts here, family influence there, to smooth things over. Now he realised that the old-boy network which had protected him so far was beginning to unravel and cold winds from across the Channel were breaking up the cosy family world of Irish politics. He had tried cooperation as long as cooperation had helped his work: now he would try defiance.

It was an unexpected decision, a courageous decision, and it involved a new development in Oliver's character. He was now one of the best known people in Irish life and he had no hope of being able to go around in disguise; he would have to go underground. Methodically, he collected his books and candles and made his plans, and on the 12th of November, 1673, he reported those plans to Propaganda.

The government here is terrified of the

anti-Catholic Parliament and dare not offer any leniency in our sentence of banishment or postpone putting it into effect beyond the 1st of December. I have urged my colleagues to stand firm and not to abandon their flocks but to follow the example of the bishops of the first three centuries and retire to some corner of their districts until the storm blows over.

I shall retire to some little hut in the woods or mountains of my diocese with a supply of candles and books. You can go on sending me letters as usual, however, and I will try to send you some information from time to time. Please be so kind as not to send envelopes as they cost me as much as the letters themselves; every letter with an envelope costs 46 bajocchi, without the envelope it would only cost 23 bajocchi.

In a postscript he added: "The Bishop of Waterford will come to my district to go into hiding, as his own city is full of fanatics and furious Presbyterians." The decision of John Brennan to travel the length of the country in order to join Oliver in Armagh is surprising and the explanation given is hardly the whole story. It looks as though Brennan, a man somewhat lacking in self-confidence, sought comfort in Oliver's companionship and strength in his leadership at this difficult time.

By mid-December the two bishops had gone to their hiding-place and from there Oliver succeeded in sending a further report to Rome. The worst news was the closing down, apparently for ever, of his dearest project, the school in Drogheda; in comparison with that, his own tribulations counted for little.

Things are very bad here and, with another meeting of Parliament due on the 7th of January next, they may get worse. I am in hiding and Dr Brennan is with me. The Catholic laity are in such great fear of having their property confiscated that no-one who has anything to lose will give shelter to any Ordinary or religious; and although the latter are being to some extent connived at, yet the Catholics hardly even dare let them into their houses to say Mass. The bishops or ordinaries can get nothing from the priests. I sometimes find it difficult even to get oaten bread; and the house where Dr Brennan and I are staying is made of straw and covered or thatched so badly that we can see the stars when we are in bed and even the lightest shower of rain sprinkles our pillows. But we are resolved to die from hunger and cold rather than abandon our flocks. It would be a shame for spiritual soldiers, educated in Rome, to become hirelings. We shall take no step without the order of Your Eminences.

The thing that has caused me the greatest sorrow is to see the destruction of the schools I founded, after so much hard work had gone into them. We have so many talented young Catholics: what are they to do now?

Worse was yet to come, as a letter dated 27th of January 1674 reported to the Internuncio in Brussels. Mgr Falconieri had no difficulty in recognising the handwriting, though for reasons of security Oliver no longer dared give either his own name or that of his companion.

About the 10th of this month the Viceroy published a further proclamation ordering that the full rigour of the law was to be applied to the clergy who had registered. Another order, this one secret, was given to all the magistrates and sheriffs to put their spies on the track of the remaining bishops and regulars, both in the cities and in the countryside.

As soon as my companion and I heard of this we thought it necessary to take to our heels. It was after vespers on Sunday, the 18th of this month (old style), the Feast of St Peter's Chair. The snow was falling heavily, mixed with hailstones which were very hard and large. There was a cutting north wind blowing into our faces and it beat the snow and hail so fiercely into our eyes that even now we are hardly able to see with them. Many times we were in danger of being lost in the valleys and of dying of suffocation in the snow.

Finally we arrived at the house of a gentleman who had lost so much he had nothing more to lose. As ill-luck would have it, however, he had a stranger staying in the house whom we did not want to recognise us, so we were placed in a large attic without either chimney or fire where we have been for the last eight days: may it all work for the glory of God and the salvation of our souls and the flocks entrusted to our charge.

The cold and the hail were so terrible that my eyes have not yet stopped running nor have those of my companion. I feel that I shall lose more than one tooth, they are paining me so much, and my companion was attacked with rheumatism in one arm and can scarcely move it.

In brief, we may truly say that our flight was in winter and on a sabbath,* that is, on Sunday, and on the Feast of St Peter's Chair. Blessed be God who granted us the favour of suffering not only for the Chair of Peter but on the very day dedicated to the feast of that chair which rests on a rock and will in the end, I hope, break the violence of these tempestuous waves.

So far I have not heard of anyone being arrested, apart from a certain Father Eugene Cogley of the Order of St Dominic, Prior of Tuam, and a Father Francis Brennan in Mullingar; but I am afraid that before long there will be so many arrests that there will be no room left in the prisons, since I have been told that the sheriffs and magistrates of the King have been ordered to hunt out the bishops and regulars and even to search private houses. God help us all.

I make you my reverence.

Thomas Cox
*27th January (old Style) 1674.*

That experience on the mountain-side, in darkness and in snow, was clearly a terrifying one. During the days that followed in the cheerless, fireless attic, Oliver had plenty of time to reflect on his close escape from death. Then came news

---

* The reference is to Matt. 24:20, "Pray that your flight may not be in winter or on a sabbath."

that Catholics in Scotland were to be liable to the
penalty of high treason. Had he escaped death
from cold and exposure in order to die a still more
painful one by the knife of the executioner? The
good shepherd laid down his life for his flock while
the hireling ran away: was this the choice he was
being asked to make? He brushed the thought
aside: under the law of the Kingdom of Ireland he
was liable to imprisonment or exile but nothing
worse. He had never been guilty of treason and
never would be.

Here we are in greater fear and trembling than
ever, for our neighbour's house is on fire. In
Scotland the Parliament enacted that in future
in should be considered high treason to hear
Mass. It would seem that the days of Nero and
Domitian and Diocletian have returned; the
penalty for this crime of high treason is to be
disembowelled and quartered. So we shall have
the blood of martyrs in abundance to fertilise
the Church. . . .
　　It is like the time of the early Church; and it
is my hope that the Church will once again be
made glorious and enriched by the sufferings
and martyrdoms of her northern children who
are humble and devoted servants and imitators
of Christ and the Apostles, and that the adverse
storm will help us even more than the favouring
breeze.
　　These edicts and proclamations and decrees
do not as yet apply to Ireland since it is not
expressly mentioned in them; but as usual I do
not think there is much danger that they will
overlook us. If they come to us, then God be

praised, we shall welcome them, whether we have to suffer or die. At all events, we shall not be hirelings. We shall not abandon the sheep or the lambs until they drag us to the boat with ropes around our necks.

I beg you to obtain for us the prayers of the servants of God, that he may protect us from the assembly of the wicked and grant us the gift of holy perseverance.

I am with all reverence your most obliged and devoted servant,

Thomas Cox
*12th February 1674.*

In the event, this particular storm abated, though neither quickly nor completely. None of the bishops was exiled that winter except Peter Talbot of Dublin, and he more for his political than for his religious activities. Having impressed the English Parliament with a great noise of anti-Catholic edicts, nearly everyone, from the Viceroy down, was content to let the matter go no further. The clergy who had registered waited in the ports while the ships were delayed by increasingly mysterious obstacles. Eventually they quietly went back to their dioceses and their religious houses. One group of friars in New Ross was actually put on board a ship and dispatched in the direction of France; but ten miles down the estuary, out of sight of the town, the friars were put on land again and rapidly disappeared from view. It was enough to make Cromwell turn in his grave.

In one sense, then, Oliver gained nothing by his miserable winter except an eye complaint that lasted the rest of his life. He could have spent the same time in comfort at Sir Nicholas Plunkett's home in Dublin, a law-abiding citizen, waiting ostentatiously for the ship that never came. But in another sense, the gains were quite incalculable. He had made the distinction between what was expedient and what was right in the clearest and most public possible terms. He had laid down the principle for himself, and through his example for others, that no Irish bishop could consent to accept exile unless bodily carried on board ship. The émigré hierarchy of the sixteen-sixties was a thing of the past: from now on Irish bishops would stay with their flocks and, if necessary, die with them.

## 8. WRITING IN FOUR LANGUAGES

Things gradually returned to something like normal, though it was not until 1675 that Oliver felt free to move around openly again. All the time the cold eye of the English Parliament was upon the Irish Papists and things that were possible a couple of years before had now become impossible again. The Drogheda schools never re-opened and Catholic education soon returned to its former unsatisfactory state. Oliver's activities seem to have become restricted in other areas too; certainly the number of his letters in the Roman archives for the years 1675 to 1679 is much less than that for the preceding period.

This may be a convenient point at which to say something about Oliver's writings. Oliver spoke four languages, English, Irish, Latin and Italian, and wrote in at least three of them (his Irish writings are of doubtful authenticity). The language in which he wrote most easily was not English but Italian, in which his twenty-three years' residence in Rome had given him great fluency. The great bulk of his letters to Rome and Brussels were written in Italian, though there were occasional letters, mostly of a more formal kind, in Latin. No-one in the Roman Curia apparently had any knowledge of English, much less Irish.

It is amazing how Oliver found time, among all his other activities, to write so many and such long letters. He wrote regularly to the other Irish bishops so as to be able to keep Propaganda informed of the whole Irish situation. He frequently sent more than one copy of an important letter, in case it was lost or intercepted on the way. He suspected Dublin Castle of tampering with his mail and his suspicions were dramatically confirmed in 1671 during an interview with Lord Berkeley. The Viceroy told him, among other things:

> That many letters of Airoldi and Baldeschi had been intercepted but that they gave great satisfaction to the government. Then he said, with emphasis: "If you follow their good advice and avoid meddling in political or civil matters, you shall have no more annoyance from the King." He also said that he had seen the printed instructions which are given to missionaries and approved of them, especially the last one, which urged them not to write about any temporal or political matters.
>
> He also said that some of my letters to Airoldi and Baldeschi had been intercepted and that he always found them making highly complimentary references to himself, for which he thanked me. I said that they contained no more than the truth. He went on to say that he had had all these letters carefully sealed and put back in the

post, and that he had given orders that no more letters of mine were to be intercepted or brought to him. I gave him infinite thanks for this, and took my leave after many expressions of politeness.

Despite the Viceroy's assurances, this extraordinary interview must have made Oliver more cautious than ever about what he wrote in his letters.

Airoldi was the Internuncio in Brussels, who had a kind of watching brief over English and Irish affairs; Baldeschi was the Secretary of the Congregation for the Propagation of the Faith, known for short as Propaganda. Oliver sent all his letters to Brussels, addressed to Airoldi under the pseudonym of M. de Pruisson, and Airoldi sent them on to Rome; similarly, Baldeschi transmitted his letters to Oliver through Airoldi. Airoldi seems to have been an amiable and tactful intermediary between the touchy Archbishop and the imperious Secretary, who did not always see eye to eye. At first, Baldeschi thought Oliver headstrong and meddlesome; snowed under by the sudden avalanche of indignant letters from Oliver's opponents, he surfaced to fire off an occasional barbed arrow in the direction of Armagh. The following may serve as an example of Baldeschi's epistolary style, its particular tone of silken insolence obviously the result of many years of practice. It is dated 27th of September, 1670.

It must be the Irish climate that has caused

Your Excellency to forget the customary forms and regulations of this Curia. I am astonished you should not remember that it is impossible for you to obtain the faculty of dismissing from their order Franciscans who have made their profession.

These lapses of memory, my dear Monsignor, are considered over here to be due to the fact that you are forgetting to apply yourself to spiritual matters as you ought and have instead become totally immersed in temporal affairs.

It would appear that Airoldi thought it prudent to forget to send on some of Baldeschi's letters and that this was one of them. In any event, Baldeschi soon came to a juster estimate of the Archbishop and, in the matter of the Tories, went so far as to admit that he was wrong and Oliver right.

On the whole, Oliver reacted fairly mildly to these and similar rebukes. Apart from his natural respect for Roman institutions, he was no doubt influenced by the fact that Baldeschi held the not inconsiderable Roman purse-strings. The Drogheda schools had been largely supported by Propaganda and there were many other expenses for which Oliver sought help from Rome. Among these was the expense of the letters themselves. A letter of 15th September, 1674, to the new Internuncio Falconieri speaks with some feeling about the matter.

If I had served the Duke of Mirandola in letter-writing and otherwise as I served the Sacred Congregation in the last five years, my baker's bill would long ago have been settled. If I had the means I would spare no pains in serving their Eminences, being bound to do so by every law of justice and gratitude; but what I cannot do, I cannot do.

Every single letter that I send to Your Excellency costs me one giulio, each letter I receive from you costs me 2½ giuli. Any time I get a letter from Cashel or Tuam it costs me a carlino in Dublin and then 2½ bajocchi from Dublin to where I live.

Then I have to pay my agents in Dublin and London, who have to go to the post to get the letters and send them on to me, and I could not be niggardly in paying them. They would not have done me this service, using their time and their shoes and their paper and their ink, if I had not been generous with them. The same is true of my correspondents in Tuam and Cashel, and indeed they were worthy of their hire.

I am sure that Your Excellency's purse also feels the expense of letters. Every year it has cost me at least 100 scudi and since you came to the Nunciature in Flanders it has cost me more than 100 scudi; because all during the persecution which has now lasted eleven months I was hidden in the mountains with the Bishop of Waterford, at least until two months ago; yet I always managed to keep up my correspondence, in spite of the difficulties.

The carlino, giulio and bajocco were small coins, but 100 scudi was equivalent to £25, a very large sum in those days. It must be remembered that there were no government postal services then such

as we have now. Letters were handled by a
network of agents, each one expecting his commission, and letters for abroad had to wait until a
ship was ready to sail. Whenever Oliver was in or
near a sea-port he took the opportunity to send off
some foreign mail. Usually this was Dublin, but on
one occasion he wrote from Galway and had to
apologise for the sorry state of the letter. "I beg
you to excuse the smears on this letter, as the
servant knocked over the bottle of ink when
making my bed. The post leaves in two hours and
is some distance away, so I have no time to re-write
the letter."

His style, like his handwriting, reads strong and
serviceable and clear. As none of his letters were
intended as literary exercises, there are no purple
patches and no striving after effect. When he had
time to compose his thoughts, he could marshal
facts and arguments in a very masterly fashion. But
usually his letters were dashed off in a hurry to
catch the post and they contain the mistakes and
disproportions and lack of order of any hastily
written document. Oliver was well aware of these
defects and one of his letters to the Internuncio
ends with the altogether charming apology, "I beg
you to excuse the prolixity of this letter, for I had
not enough time to make it shorter." At first
reading one imagines that he has made a mistake,
then one realises that he means exactly what he
says.

Little need be said about his writings in Latin,
which are mainly short formal documents; his
Latin is correct but awkward, with little feeling for

the language. But he shows familiarity with the works of the masters of Latin literature and quotes from Virgil, Horace, Ovid and Boethius. All his scripture quotations and references are given in the Latin of the Vulgate version, whether the rest of the letter is in Italian or in English; and since scriptural allusions abound in his writings, one comes across a Latin phrase or sentence every few lines.

His writing in English is noticeably less fluent than in Italian. This is surprising, since he presumably spoke English from his earliest years; in all likelihood he spoke English to his family and social equals, Irish to servants and tenants. During his long years in Rome, however, he probably wrote little in either language and lost some of his facility. In the introduction to his book on the primacy, he makes the request to the reader "that you expect not in this treatise the style of an orator well versed in the English tongue, wherein I acknowledge my weakness, but regard the substance of the subject matter in question". The style of the book is better than this would lead one to expect, rugged but clear, but his sentences tend to become long and involved in a manner more suggestive of Latin than of modern English.

Anyhow, for Oliver style was an irrelevancy. The important thing was what was said, not how it was said. In a postscript to one of the last letters he ever wrote, he apologised to Father Corker for his rough style; but the apology has a ring of pride about it.

My language and words are rude. I never hunted after flourishes in any language. Words are signs, *sunt enim signa seu notae eorum conceptuum seu passionum quae sunt in animo\**, as the philosopher saith. Many taverns have fair and majestical signs though there be no good liquor in the cellar. But I know you are like those travellers who had rather enter to an inn furnished with good wine, though it had but a withered ill-shaped sign, than to lodge at a tavern full of corrupted and adulterated liquors, although adorned with a lofty, gilded, and fairly painted sign, whose sight allures all passengers to light but they never return again; and even as gallant signs doth not feed the passenger's belly, so words do not feed the hearer's or reader's brain or understanding, who is by solid enthymemes and syllogisms comforted and nourished.

Finally some mention must be made of Oliver's writing in Irish. Nothing survives in his own handwriting, but there are two quatrains which have been attributed to him. One is a rather bitter epigram on the priests of the time:

Sagairt óir is cailís chrainn
   Bhi le linn Phádraig i n-Éirinn;
Sagairt chrainn is cailís óir
   I ndeire an domhain dearóil.

Priests of gold and chalices of wood
   Were Ireland's' lot in Patrick's time of old;

---

\* They are signs or marks of those concepts and passions which are in the mind.

But now the latter days of our sad world
    Have priests of wood and chalices of
    gold.

If not actually written by him, these lines may well have been quoted by him. Events certainly gave him cause for a somewhat jaundiced view of the contemporary priesthood.

The other four-line stanza is addressed to Tara, where the palace of the High King of ancient Ireland once stood. It was written on seeing a peasant cutting grass on that venerable site, and may form part of a longer poem.

    A Theamhair na rí, dob annamh leat,
        Re linn Chormaic mhic Airt mhic Cuinn,
    Alt riabhach do bhodach bhocht
        Bheith ag gearra guirt ar do dhruim.

    Tara of Kings, how strange for thee,
        In Cormac Mac Art's far distant day,
    To feel upon thy back the fist
        Of some rough peasant cutting hay.

These lines, if they are genuine, show that Oliver had more feeling for the history and traditions of Gaelic Ireland than his birth and upbringing would suggest.

# 9. THE STORM GATHERS

The uneasy peace continued in Ireland, though London seethed with rumour and intrigue. Tension grew between the King and the Parliament, and the King's opponents found an able and unscrupulous leader in the Earl of Shaftesbury. Shaftesbury was not particularly anti-Catholic but he was happy to use any weapon, however dishonourable, to break the power of the monarchy. The King's wife and brother were Catholics and the King was only waiting a favourable opportunity of becoming a Catholic himself; so it was clear enough to Shaftesbury that by playing on the anti-Catholic suspicions of the mob he could easily arouse them against the royal family. A variety of fantastic rumours were put into circulation, anti-Popery demonstrations were organised, and the Catholics were accused of having caused everything from the execution of Charles I to the Great Fire of London.

Some time early in the year 1676 a down-at-heel clergyman by the name of Titus Oates arrived in London. Though still in his twenties, he had already had various brushes with the law for crimes ranging from perjury to sodomy. He was as repulsive in body as he was in mind, squat, bull-necked, bow-legged, with a voice like the braying of a donkey. His complexion was vermilion in colour, his eyes sunken and pig-like, and his chin so large that it almost equalled all the rest of his face put together. "His mouth was the centre of his face," wrote one of his contemporaries, "and a compass there would sweep his nose, forehead, and chin within the perimeter."

For many months Oates led a hand-to-mouth existence, during which time he was befriended and helped by a few of London's poor Catholics. He expressed a desire to become a Catholic himself and was received into the Church in March, 1677. He then discovered in himself a vocation to the Jesuit priesthood and eventually succeeded in getting himself admitted to the secondary school run by the English Jesuits at St Omer, in Belgium, as a pupil. He lasted there some six months, from December 1677 to June 1678, a twenty-eight-years-old oddity among the schoolboys, before being expelled and sent back to London as unfit even to be considered for the Jesuit novitiate. The night before he left, he was found in the chapel, leaning on the altar in the attitude of the priest at the consecration of the Mass. When asked what he was doing, he replied, "I am bidding farewell to Jesus Christ."

That six months in St Omer, combined with his Catholic contacts in London, was all that Oates needed. He sat down and in cold blood fabricated the entire "Popish Plot". It was to make his name immortal, and deservedly, for no more monstrous invention has ever bubbled from the mind of man. Unlike the discoverers of previous plots, Oates knew a good deal about the English Jesuits, their work, their organisation, their names. He skilfully blended fact and fiction into a long narrative, bristling with people and places and dates, and succeeded in getting the document brought before the King's Privy Council. On the 28th of September he was summoned to appear before the Council in person and there he re-affirmed all the lies written in his narrative and added a few more in the inspiration of the moment. The Council listened in amazement as he detailed the horrid conspiracy for them. The King was to be murdered and his brother put on the throne. The Protestant religion was to be proscribed and leading Protestants put to death. The Scottish Presbyterians were to be incited to revolt. In Ireland a Popish army of twenty thousand horse and twenty thousand foot was ready to rise in rebellion and a French army would be sent to help them. Immediate and drastic action was needed if England was not to be reduced to a helpless vassal of Rome.

The years spent by Titus Oates in concocting the Popish Plot had been years of quiet consolidation for Oliver Plunkett. His diocese, he reported to the Internuncio, was now "completely at peace, except for two priests who are refractory". He continued his work of visitation and administered the sacraments of confirmation and ordination. According to the careful lists he kept, he had confirmed

48,655 people up to the outbreak of the persecution of 1673, some in places which had seen no bishop for forty years. Now the crowds presenting themselves for confirmation were smaller and the clerical disputes less frequent. In 1676 he even allowed himself the luxury of a holiday and went to spend a few weeks with his friend, John Brennan, in Waterford.

The only real disturbance during these years happened in the diocese of Kilmore, within the province of Armagh, which involved the Vicar-General and some of the clergy and which dragged on from 1676 to 1678. It would be wearisome to describe it, except to say that Oliver was called in and gave his judgment against the Vicar-General, a judgment which was eventually confirmed by Rome. The defeated faction sent the usual stream of complaints and accusations to Rome: Oliver was dictatorial, he favoured the Anglo-Irish at the expense of the native Irish, he used his political influence to have some priests arrested, he was too friendly with the Protestants. Asked by Rome to investigate the charges, John Brennan found that only the last had any truth in it.

As regards the accusation that the Archbishop of Armagh is giving scandal to Catholics by being over friendly with Protestant ministers, I must say that during all the time I have been in this country, I never heard of any such scandal. If by Protestant ministers they mean ministers of the Protestant Church, it is true that he is friendly with one minister, an official of the so-called primate; but this friendship is greatly to the advantage of his flock, for whenever any lawsuits involving Catholics, especially marriage cases, are brought to the Protestant Episcopal Court, this minister sends them on to Dr Plunkett. I have not heard of his being friendly with any other minister of the Protestant Church.

If by Protestant ministers they mean magistrates and ministers of court, it is true that he is friendly with many of them and they are of great help to him, because it means that they can from their own personal knowledge reject the accusations brought against him through the ill-will of clerics and laymen. Were it not for his friendship with these men, he would probably have been banished long ago from the Kingdom like the Archbishops of Dublin and Tuam, so great is the malevolence of these informers.

Brennan may have under-estimated Oliver's friendship with Protestant ministers: it is clear from other letters that Oliver had friendly contacts with the Protestant Archbishop of Armagh and Bishop of Clogher. But the real rub was that Oliver was still a Palesman, a speaker of English, a bearer of Norman blood, with an entry to the corridors of power that none of the old Irish could any longer command. For some of the old Irish this was and always would be Oliver's unforgivable sin. They did not want this man to rule over them.

Oliver was now in his early fifties, a fairly advanced age by the standards of those days. The years of constant travel and hardship had taken their toll of him, both in body and in spirit; a letter of 1677 speaks of the humiliation of the Irish bishops in their journeys: "they have to go today to the house of one gentleman for their meals and tomorrow to another's, which is shameful for the bishops and wearisome for the gentry". By August, 1678, his eye-trouble had become quite severe.

> The last two months were spent in making a difficult and tiring visitation of my diocese, of which I shall shortly give a full account to Your Excellency.... The journey through the mountains of the northern districts was very fatiguing and it made the running from my eyes much worse so that I can hardly write or read letters even if they are as large as a snuff-box. Still, it did not stop my tongue from preaching both in English and in Irish.

He had given everything he had to the service of his God and of his Church, everything except his life. Now that sacrifice too was to be asked of him.

In August, 1678, no-one had heard of the name of Titus Oates. By the end of September his name was on everybody's lips. The Popish Plot had been an unbelievable success.

Historians are still trying to explain the frenzy that gripped England for the next three years. It owed something to the strange personality of Oates, whose capacity for spontaneous invention is without parallel in human history. It owed something also to the skilful stage-management of Lord Shaftesbury, who lost no time in taking Oates under his wing and using him for his own ends. It was fuelled by the murder of a London magistrate, whose death was at once attributed to the Jesuits, and it was augmented by the droves of perjured witnesses who flocked to share in Oates's glittering spoils. The arch-perjurer himself had been transformed from a penniless vagabond into the most adulated man in the Kingdom, with a royal pension, a suite of rooms in the Palace of Whitehall, and the title "Saviour of the Nation".

In London and in many parts of England Catholic priests and laymen were hunted down and imprisoned. The series of trials began which was to lead to the execution of many completely innocent people and to write the most disgraceful chapter in all the annals of English justice. Corrupt and hectoring judges, packed juries, and a mob of shouting and jeering spectators made any kind of defence impossible. The verdict "Guilty" was a foregone conclusion and the gallows at Tyburn claimed the lives of some of the best men in England.

The political results were equally gratifying. The King, though he knew he was the ultimate objective of the whole attack, felt himself powerless to deal with the situation; he signed the death warrants of his most loyal supporters and granted pensions and rewards to their false accusers. The King's brother, the Duke of York, was forced to leave England altogether and live in exile in Brussels. The Queen, who knew some of the priest-victims personally and hung their portraits in her room, was accused by the insufferable Oates of plotting to poison her husband.

Only one thing was wanting to the full success of the Plot. None of the victims confessed to the crimes of which they were found guilty. This was a blow to the credibility of Oates and his hirelings and they made every effort to extort a confession from the condemned men, even offering them their lives if they admitted their guilt. It was in vain: without exception, they proclaimed their innocence with their last breath. It was one of the things that would eventually turn the tide against the Plot, but not for some time yet.

From Ireland, Oliver Plunkett watched events in England with anxiety. Ireland now had a new viceroy, the Duke of Ormond, replacing the Earl of Essex, who had joined Shaftesbury in opposition to the King. Ormond, the leading Irish nobleman of the time, had no love for Catholics; but he knew as did everyone else in Ireland, that the Irish part of the Plot with its Popish army of 40,000 men was completely without foundation. In addition, he had many links by blood and marriage with the Plunketts; he was unlikely to take any action against Oliver of his own free will. But to protect his own position he had to be seen to take some action. He ordered the arrest of the Archbishop of Dublin, Peter Talbot, who had recently returned from exile a dying man, and who had the misfortune of having been named in Oates's narrative; and he followed this with a new edict of banishment.

Once again Oliver prepared to go underground,

and he wrote from Dublin to inform the Inter-nuncio of the situation on the 27th of October, 1678.

The Provincial Council had suggested that I should make a visitation of the province, so I began with Meath, the first suffragan diocese, and then went on to Clonmacnois. I had just finished there when the news came by post that Dr Talbot of Dublin had been arrested, and imprisoned in the Castle or Tower of this city. I heard this on the 21st of this month. Im-mediately after that a proclamation or edict was issued banishing all the archbishops, bishops, vicar-generals, and all the regular clergy, ordering them to leave the Kingdom before the 20th of November, and threatening fines and penalties against anyone found giving them food or drink or helping them in any way.

I was quite astonished at the arrest of the Archbishop of Dublin, especially as he had not performed any ecclesiastical function since his return to Ireland. The houses of the unfortunate regulars have been closed and the clergy scat-tered: so the edict puts an end to all the disputes and the plans for reform. The parish priests and secular clergy are not included in it. It is not known what exactly the Archbishop of Dublin is being charged with; he is being held in the secret prison and no-one can communicate with him.

A number of people have been arrested in London for conspiring against the King, for corresponding secretly with foreign rulers, and for the murder of a nobleman who was found dead in London. As for the plot against the King, it is a complete invention.

I have not been included by name in the

present edict, nor was I in the one of four years ago; so I will stay on in the kingdom, but inconspicuously in some country place. Dr Brennan will probably be with me. I heard this morning that Dr Talbot will be sent to London for trial: whatever happens, endurance will conquer all adversity.

From now on, be good enough to address your letters thus: "For Mr Edward Hamon, Dublin"; and I will no longer write to Your Excellency under the name of Monsieur Pruisson, but as Monsieur Picquet à Bruxelles.

How Oliver spent the winter of 1678-79, his second winter as a fugitive, we are not told. He may have been unable to send letters or they may have been intercepted on the way. The next the Internuncio heard of him was a letter of the 15th of May, 1679:

Things here are going from bad to worse. First the prelates and regulars were ordered into exile, now they are turning on the parish priests and several of them have been put in prison. If a fair-minded Protestant shows them any kindness, he is called a Papist by the others, which is regarded as a great insult. Colonel Fitzpatrick, an excellent Catholic though a relative of the Duke of Ormond, was banished from Court, and in London they are trying to bring charges against the Duke of York himself.

A reward has already been offered to spies and constables and soldiers, 40 crowns for the arrest of a prelate and 20 for a regular. I am morally certain of being captured, there are so many hunting for me. But, whatever the danger, I will stay with my flock and will not abandon them until I am dragged to the ship.

However, in case I am captured, I would like you to tell me where I should go; they have given others a choice, I am sure they will do the same to me. Please let me have your advice or recommendation on this, whether I should go to France or Flanders or somewhere else.

## 10. THE ARREST OF MR MELEADY

For another six months Oliver enjoyed a precarious liberty. Although he did not know it, he was still being shielded by Ormond's goodwill. It was not until the end of October that Ormond finally issued orders for his arrest at the express command of the Privy Council in London. The Council had been informed that Oliver was involved in a plot to set up a French army for the invasion of Ireland and they wanted him arrested and questioned. Ormond was not prepared to risk his position by dragging his feet any longer and he immediately set his spies on the track of the Primate as a matter of the utmost urgency.

Before long, he had some definite information to go on. Oliver had been seen staying near the Naul, a village a few miles north of Dublin, under the name of Mr Meleady; he had cut off his beard and moustache and was wearing a wig. The wig is not so dramatic as it sounds; it was customary for gentlemen of quality to wear a periwig and to go clean-shaven. Oliver was no longer of an age when he could carry off the role of an army officer; the name Mr Meleady suggests elderly respectability and the disguise went with it. His presence near Dublin was probably explained by the fact that his old friend and tutor Patrick Plunkett was dying, full of years and honour, in the seventy-sixth year of his age.

On the 30th of November Oliver was still at liberty. On that day he wrote to Rome to inform them that the aged bishop had at last gone to his reward.

> I must give you the sad news of the death of Dr Patrick Plunkett, Bishop of Meath, a prelate distinguished by his birth, his sincerity, his integrity of life, his skill and experience in matters ecclesiastical, and his devotion to his duties as a bishop for thirty-three long years.... He died poor because he lived rich, generous in his alms-giving. His right hand did not know what his left hand was doing. He never denied charity to anyone in need and he gave many gifts in secret to those who were ashamed to let their poverty be known, to respectable men and to widows, of whom we have a large number since the massacre of Cromwell.

On the 6th of December, 1679, Oliver Plunkett was arrested. It is not known how or where, except that it was somewhere in or around Dublin. He was taken to Dublin Castle and there lodged in the secret prison, in the next cell to the Archbishop of Dublin. For six weeks he was held incommunicado in solitary confinement while his papers were examined in vain for something that appeared even remotely treasonable. It was not until the 17th of

January, 1680, that he was given the opportunity of writing to Rome and giving some information about his situation.

> May the Lord be praised, who has given me two reasons for spiritual rejoicing. The first is my imprisonment in this tower or royal castle, where I was held in strict confinement from the 6th of December until yesterday, when I was given permission to speak with some friends and my servants; this was because they examined my papers and found nothing about politics or temporal affairs, with which I never concerned myself. The second is the news of the calumnies of an apostate friar, Anthony Daly, bosom friend of Father Felim O'Neill.

The rest of the long letter is a point by point answer to accusations made against him by Daly, the Franciscan friar who had allegedly sent the Tories to assassinate Oliver six years previously. For the last year he had been bombarding officials in Rome and Brussels with allegations about the Primate's misdeeds. Many of the incidents and names he mentioned are as obscure to us as they were to the Roman officials, but some of the charges were manifestly absurd, such as that Oliver had deliberately instigated the recent persecutions in order to rid himself of his enemies. ("This calumniator says that I alone am in favour while others are persecuted," wrote Oliver. "How is it then that I am in prison and they are free?") There is almost a tone of despair about Oliver's letter, as if he had given up hope of ever catching up with the slanders against him. It is saddening and shaming to read his attempts to clear his name with Rome, a prisoner already marked down for death.

At this stage, Oliver probably did not realise the danger he was in. He had broken the law of *Praemunire*, and had resisted the decree of banishment, but the punishment for these offences was not death; he still expected to be deported to some place on the Continent of Europe. It was only gradually that he came to realise that he was being set up as the prime mover of the Irish branch of the Popish Plot and that Shaftesbury and Oates had sent agents to find witnesses against him. They found two among the disaffected clergy of Oliver's own diocese. One was Edmund Murphy, who had been parish priest of Killeavy until suspended from his position by the Primate. The other was John McMoyer, a Franciscan from the Armagh friary, one of the two who had beheaded Oliver's bust in Rome.

During the spring and summer of 1680 Oliver remained in Dublin Castle while the case was being built up against him. His conditions had improved a little. He had a cell with a small balcony on which he was allowed to walk and take the air, and was allowed to have his servant, James McKenna, with him. For these privileges he had to pay £1 a week. His jailers seem to have been reasonably humane and his friends were allowed to send him in food.

In the next cell, Peter Talbot was slowly dying. Whatever rivalry had existed between the two was forgotten in a dramatic incident which occurred at this time. Dr Mark Forristal, the newly appointed bishop of Kildare, reported it to Rome in a letter of the 5th of June, written in unusually elegant Latin.

> The unfortunate Archbishop of Dublin is suffering from an illness which affects his brain and his whole body and on last Friday the good man very nearly breathed his last. Despite the reluctance of the jailers, the Primate forced his way in to him in order to console him and give him absolution. The Primate himself, in the same prison, is uncertain of his fate and of his future. He is in the strictest confinement because he has been the subject of false accusations by good-for-nothing ruffians and, shameful to say, treacherous priests, who are trying to revenge themselves on him.

Talbot lingered on for a few more months before death released him from his prison cell. Whether the two archbishops ever met again we are not told.

The Viceroy ordered Oliver's trial to be held in Dundalk towards the end of July. This was greatly to Oliver's advantage, as he was well known to everyone in the area. It was disastrous for his two accusers, who were also well known there as former inmates of the town jail. What followed was described in detail by Oliver in a letter of the 25th of July.

> I was brought under guard to Dundalk on the 21st of July; Dundalk is about 36 miles from

Dublin. I was put into the custody of the King's Lieutenant for that district, who treated me with great courtesy.

On the 23rd and 24th of July I had to appear in court. A long list of charges was read but McMoyer failed to appear on the 24th to confirm his statements and answer my defence. I had thirty-two witnesses, priests, friars and laymen, all prepared to refute everything the friar had sworn: namely, that I had seventy thousand Catholics prepared to murder all the Protestants and to establish here the Romish religion and Popish superstition; that I had sent various agents to different kingdoms to obtain aid; that I had visited and explored all the fortresses and maritime ports of the kingdom; and that I had held a provincial council in 1678 to introduce the French. He had also in his sworn statements made accusations against Monsignor Tyrrell, the Reverend Luke Plunkett, and Dr Edward Dromgoole, an eminent preacher.

The other witness, Murphy, fled from the kingdom when he heard that the trial was to be held in Dundalk; McMoyer claimed that he could not come forward himself as he was waiting for Murphy to return; and so the trial ended. According to the law of this country I must attend three assizes before I can be acquitted, and as there will not be another assizes in Dundalk until the end of next March my counsel and friends have advised me to present a petition to have the case heard in Dublin at the next assizes at All Saints and to have the Dundalk jury brought to Dublin. It is possible I may succeed in having this granted to me.

The method of procedure in criminal cases here seems quite extraordinary to me. The defendant knows nothing of the charges against him until the day of his trial, he is not allowed a counsel to defend him, his witnesses cannot take the oath, and one witness is sufficient to make the case for the Crown. The witnesses for the defence, however, are allowed to give evidence but not under oath.

After the sitting I was brought back by the Viceroy's orders to Dublin Castle, to my costly and expensive apartment. But Dundalk was even more expensive, even though I spent such a short time there, because I had to bring thirty-two witnesses from different parts and pay their expenses for four days in Dundalk, and I distributed about 40 crowns among the guards and servants of the Lieutenant.

Although the two chief judges are appointed by the Crown, the Lieutenant of the district of Dundalk chooses the jury. As there are more Catholics than Protestants in the County of Louth, McMoyer knew that there would surely be some Catholics on the jury; he also knew that the Lieutenant, officially called the Sheriff, was a friend of mine; so he presented a petition that no Catholic should be on the jury and this was granted to him. I raised no objection to this, as I knew that all the Protestants of my district looked upon McMoyer as an accomplice of the Tories, for which he was prosecuted and fined at the Armagh sessions in 1678. I also knew that they all regarded the accusations McMoyer made against me as wild inventions. Moreover, his dissolute life was notorious and he was always half drunk when he appeared in court.

The reason why Murphy fled was because he knew full well that the jury in Dundalk would have hanged him. He had been in prison in Dundalk and escaped. He had been found in the company of the Tories and had concealed their stolen goods.

It was only at this abortive trial in Dundalk that Oliver realised what kind of charges were being made against him, charges that carried the death penalty if proved. He knew, however, that no jury in Ireland would find him guilty of such absurdities. Unfortunately, Shaftesbury now realised the same thing and he set to work to have the trial transferred to London. Ormond protested that it was unprecedented and illegal for anyone to be tried in England for a crime committed in Ireland, but Shaftesbury managed to produce one very shaky precedent and Ormond was over-ruled. On the 24th of October Oliver was taken from Dublin Castle and put on board ship for England. Five days later he was lodged in Newgate prison in London.

# 11. THE COURT OF KING'S BENCH

For the next six months, while Oliver remained in solitary confinement, Shaftesbury and Oates worked hard on the Irish plot. The English plot was by now showing signs of wear and tear and some distressing incidents had recently occurred. Among these was the acquittal of one or two of those accused by the Saviour of the Nation, including a distinguished Benedictine priest, Father Maurus Corker. Father Corker was still in prison in Newgate but the fact that he and others were alive at all cast a slur on the reputation of Oates and his allies. A really blood-curdling Irish plot was the best hope for retrieving the situation but witnesses were needed to give evidence of its existence.

There was no shortage of candidates. Ireland had more than its share of criminals in that disturbed period and they began to flock to London in search of reward and, even more important, pardon for past offences. Evil-looking characters in leather jackets and brogues hung around Oates's apartments in Whitehall and Shaftesbury's elegant house in Aldersgate Street. The difficulty was to find someone among them who could tell a coherent story in court. When sober, they could hardly speak comprehensible English; when drunk, as they generally seemed to be, they were incapable of anything beyond uttering rude cries in Erse. Even the repulsive Oates found it difficult to stomach the company of these jailbirds, horse-thieves and highwaymen, and when denouncing his royalist opponents in England he could find no worse term of abuse than to compare them to Irish Tories. By a strange quirk of history the epithet stuck, and the English Conservative party is known as the Tory party to this day.

Eventually, the list was narrowed down and the successful candidates were rehearsed in their recitations. To McMoyer and Murphy a third priest was added. He was Hugh Duffy, a Franciscan, who had been McMoyer's partner in the Rome escapade and later became Murphy's curate in Killeavy, where his parish duties seemed to include robbery with violence. This trio of desperadoes formed a firm nucleus; with the addition of half a dozen or so supporting players, they were adjudged fit to appear before the Grand Jury, the body which had to decide what cases were to be brought to trial. Their first appearance in February was a disaster and they contradicted one another hopelessly; but a second attempt, after another two months of rehearsal, was more successful. The Grand Jury ordered that the Primate be brought before the Court of King's Bench on the 3rd of May, 1681.

From October, 1680 until May, 1681 Oliver had been kept in solitary confinement in Newgate prison. During that long winter, one of the coldest in living memory, he never saw a friendly face or heard a friendly voice. His faithful servant, James McKenna, accompanied him to London in the hope of being able to attend on him as he had done in Dublin; but when he tried to bring him some clean linen in the prison, he was himself arrested and locked up in another part of the jail. The filth of the prison was indescribable, the food uneatable, and the prisoners had to wear irons on their ankles, joined together by a heavy chain. Oliver's health was failing rapidly, and his hair was almost snow white. Shortly after his arrival he was described in the prison records as being "very ancient and subject to divers infirmities". Three months later he was suffering "by reason of his close confinement, and want of assistance for the distemper of the stone and gravel, which often afflicts him".

That terrible winter in Newgate was the dark night of the soul for the Archbishop of Armagh. It was his testing time, the purifying fire from which he emerged with a new strength and clarity. In the plan of his life, those months of pain and isolation were the time when he was to reach his full stature, the Gethsemane which prepared him for the climb to Calvary. It was only in his last days on earth, after serving that grim tertianship, that he showed how great a man he was, or how great a man he had become. He showed a deep spirituality that had not been seen before, perhaps because the circumstances were not there to reveal it. But he also showed qualities which suggested that he had reached a new and final stage in his voyaging, a serenity, a transparence, a simplicity, a humility, a renouncing of his own will and a willingness to submit to the will of others, that had not been his before. The fettering of his body was the freeing of his spirit. In that fetid cell, in those days and weeks when he prayed without ceasing and to the rigours of his prison added penances of his own, he came at last to a complete understanding and a complete mastery of himself.

Among Oliver's fellow-prisoners was Father Maurus Corker, found not guilty of treason but still confined. Because of his acquittal, he was allowed more freedom than other prisoners and he soon made it his business to find out everything he could about the imprisoned primate. Afterwards he was to write down his recollections of the martyr, and of this period he wrote:

> After his transportation hither he was, as you know, close confined and secluded from all human conversation save that of his keepers until his arraignment, so that here also I am much in the dark and can only inform you of what I learnt as it were by chance from the mouths of the said keepers, viz., that he spent his time in almost continual prayer, that he fasted usually three or four days a week with nothing but bread, that he appeared to them always modestly cheerful without any anguish or concern at his danger or strict confinement, that by his sweet and pious demeanour he attracted an esteem and reverence from those few that came near him.

On the 3rd of May Oliver made his first appearance before the Court of King's Bench. It was a formal proceeding, for the reading of the charges against the prisoner and the fixing of a date for his trial. The judges decided that the trial should be held on the 8th of June, a bare five weeks away. The prisoner objected that it was illegal to try anyone in England for a crime supposedly committed in Ireland; his objection was over-ruled. He asked for a longer time than five weeks so that he could bring over his witnesses from Ireland; his request was rejected. The Court also refused to let him have a priest visit him, but agreed to let him see his servant, James McKenna, only recently released from jail.

The re-union between the Archbishop and his servant was a brief one. Almost immediately McKenna, accompanied by a relative of Oliver's, set out for Ireland in the all but hopeless task of rounding up the witnesses in the short time permitted them. Everything turned out against them; contrary winds at Holyhead delayed them, the Dublin authorities refused to give them copies of the criminal records of the prosecution witnesses, and held up the issuing of safe-conducts for the defence witnesses. McKenna went back to London to bring the news: the Archbishop's witnesses were on the way but there was now no possibility of their arriving in time for the trial.

The trial of Oliver Plunkett was held in Westminster Hall, London, on the 8th of June, 1681. All the trappings of justice were lavishly displayed, only justice itself was lacking. At one end of the great hall on a raised platform sat the three judges in their gold chains and scarlet robes, headed by the Lord Chief Justice himself, Sir Francis Pemberton. There were no less than five counsels for the prosecution, among them Sir George Jeffreys who soon after immortalised himself as Judge Jeffreys of the Bloody Assizes, notorious even in an age of legal bullies. There was a jury of twelve good men and true, handpicked by Shaftesbury's agents. There was the people of England, represented by the London mob, who normally hooted and pelted the defence witnesses in the Popish Plot trials: a pleasure which would be denied them today, since the defence witnesses had only just landed in Holyhead. There was the prisoner standing alone, compelled to conduct his own defence without any counsel to speak for him, without any fore-knowledge of the charges to be brought against him, without any means even of noting down the various allegations which he would later be expected to answer.

The account of the day's proceedings was soon afterwards printed in pamphlet form, as was the custom of the time; but the account was edited to favour the prosecution and discredit the defence. Even in that unsatisfactory condition, it still reads as a sad and shabby travesty of justice, a meaningless parading of the forms of legal process without the content.

The proceedings opened with another appeal from the prisoner for time to get his witnesses to London, which met with another rebuff. Then the prosecution stated their case. They would bring witnesses to prove that the prisoner had been appointed Primate by the Pope in order to raise an army in Ireland and overthrow the government, that for this purpose he forced the Irish clergy to raise money and make a census of all able-bodied men in the country, and that he toured the harbours of Ireland to find a suitable landing-place for a French invasion, finally settling on Carlingford in County Louth as the best for the purpose.

Nine witnesses in all appeared for the prosecution. In addition to the three priests from Armagh, five laymen and a Clogher priest had been pressed into service. These were supporting players with little to say beyond vague hearsay rumours of plots and letters and mysterious meetings, and their main function was to build up an atmosphere of conspiracy and intrigue. The hard work of pinning the guilt on the Archbishop of Armagh was to be left to the three principals.

The first of the three to speak was the Franciscan, Hugh Duffy. He performed well for his employers, relating with circumstantial detail how he heard the prisoner engaging in treasonable plotting with the Bishop of Clogher and accompanied him on a reconnoitring trip to Carlingford. He had also seen letters from the prisoner looking for money for the rebel army. He was not disconcerted when the prisoner asked him to produce the letters. "I could have brought them but thought it needless," he replied loftily.

Edmund Murphy was a different case. As a secular priest of the diocese of Armagh, he owed most loyalty to the Primate and his treachery was the greatest. He was expected to repeat the story he had learnt off for the Grand Jury, of how Oliver had been appointed Primate by the Pope on condition that he would raise a rebellion in Ireland; but faced with his own conscience and seeing his Archbishop already marked down for death, he could not go through with it and began to mumble and hedge.

ATTORNEY GENERAL:
Answer my question: have you ever been with Plunkett in Ireland?
MURPHY:
Yes, sir.
ATTORNEY GENERAL:
Have you ever heard him own himself Primate of Ireland?
MURPHY:
Yes, Titular Primate.
ATTORNEY GENERAL:
Under whom did he claim that authority? Under the king or under the pope?
MURPHY:
I think he could not be under the king at all.
ATTORNEY GENERAL:
Under whom then?
MURPHY:
It must be either the king or the pope.
LORD CHIEF JUSTICE:
Answer me directly, did he claim to be titular head under the pope?
MURPHY:
I suppose he did.
LORD CHIEF JUSTICE:
Was he reputed generally so to be?

MURPHY:

Yes, my lord.

ATTORNEY-GENERAL:

Mr Murphy, remember what you swore before the Grand Jury. Pray recollect yourself whether that be true, and tell all.

LORD CHIEF JUSTICE:

You are upon your oath, you must speak the truth and the whole truth. You must not mince or conceal anything.

SERJEANT JEFFREYS:

Did you give in any evidence to the Grand Jury?

MURPHY:

Yes, I did.

SERJEANT JEFFREYS:

Was what you swore before the Grand Jury true, upon your oath?

MURPHY:

I can't say but it was.

SERJEANT JEFFREYS:

Repeat it. Tell my lord and the jury what it was, and tell the truth.

MURPHY:

I have forgot it.

Despite further attempts by the Bench and Counsel to jog his memory, Murphy remained unhelpful. "It is evident," said the Lord Chief Justice, "that the Catholics have been tampering with him." To which Jeffreys replied, "I desire he may be committed, my lord, because he hath fenced from the beginning." Accordingly, Murphy was committed to prison for contempt of court.

Fortunately for the prosecution, John McMoyer

was at hand to pick up the pieces after this disaster. He was the most fluent of all the witnesses and he never hesitated as he described totally imaginary conversations with the Primate in Armagh and equally imaginary letters written by him to Rome, none of which were produced. The only awkwardness occurred when Oliver tried to shake the witness's credibility by drawing attention to his criminal past. The Lord Chief Justice himself had to come to McMoyer's rescue. "Look you, Mr Plunkett," he said, "don't misspend your own time; for the more you trifle in these things, the less time you will have for your defence." He knew, of course, that attacking the credibility of the prosecution witnesses was the only defence that the prisoner had left to him.

After the closing speeches, the Lord Chief Justice summarised the evidence for the jury. "I leave it to you," he concluded. "It is pretty strong evidence. He does not say anything to it, but that his witnesses are not come over." The jury retired and were back again in a quarter of an hour.

CLERK OF THE CROWN:
Oliver Plunkett, hold up thy hand. How say you, is he guilty of the high treason whereof he stands indicted or not guilty?
FOREMAN:
Guilty.
PLUNKETT:
Deo gratias, God be thanked.

The Court rose, the hall emptied, and the prisoner was brought back to his cell in Newgate.

By the custom of the time, a week elapsed between the end of the trial and the passing of the sentence. The penalty for high treason was death and this was the penalty that Oliver faced, unless he were granted a reprieve. The King had the power to reprieve but had never had the courage to exercise it for any of the Popish Plot victims, though he was fully aware of their innocence; there was little chance that he would intervene now, even though he was being subjected to unusual pressure.

The outcome of the Archbishop's trial had caused horror not only in Ireland but all over Europe. The Pope urged the Catholic monarchs to do everything in their power to help him. The ambassadors of Austria, Spain and France were instructed to make representations to the English government. The French ambassador reported that Charles said he was more sorry than he could possibly express to see an innocent man condemned but was afraid to grant a reprieve in the circumstances of the time.

Another and quite unexpected intervention came from the Earl of Essex, the former Irish Viceroy, who was now living in London and had joined Shaftesbury in opposition to the King. He went to Charles to assure him of Oliver's innocence and ask for a pardon. Not surprisingly, the King lost his temper. "Why did you not attest this at his trial?" he asked angrily. "It would have done him some good then. I dare not pardon anyone. His blood be upon your head, not mine."

There was one other way in which Oliver could

escape the gallows. None of the Plot victims had
confessed to their guilt, even though offered their
lives if they did. When Richard Langhorne, the
Jesuits' lawyer, had been condemned to death,
Shaftesbury himself had gone to Newgate to offer
him life and fortune in exchange for a confession;
but in vain. Now the same offer was made to
Oliver.

It was no spirit of benevolence that prompted it.
Shaftesbury was now in serious difficulty. For
many thoughtful people, in England as well as
abroad, the Plunkett trial had been the last straw.
The sordid and cynical farce had convinced them
not only of the Archbishop's innocence but of the
innocence of all those others who had suffered in
the name of the same conspiracy. The whole
rickety fabric of lies and perjuries was beginning to
fall apart and the revulsion caused by the Archbishop's death would complete its ruin. The only
thing that could save it was for Oliver to admit his
guilt.

The offer was made and rejected. Nothing now
stood between Oliver and the sentence of death.

The prisoner made his third and last appearance
before the Court of King's Bench on the 15th of
June. Before the sentence was passed, he had to
endure a long lecture from the Lord Chief Justice
which began with a vicious attack upon his
religion.

LORD CHIEF JUSTICE:
Look you, Mr Plunkett, you have been here

indicted of a very great and heinous crime, the greatest and most heinous of all crimes, and that is, high treason; and truly yours is treason of the highest nature, it is a treason in truth against God and your king, and the country where you lived.

You have done as much as you could to dishonour our God in this case; for the bottom of your treason was your setting up your false religion, than which there is not anything more displeasing to God or pernicious to mankind in the world. A religion that is ten times worse than all the heathenish superstitions; the most dishonourable and derogatory to God and his glory of all religions or pretended religions whatsoever, for it undertakes to dispense with God's laws and to pardon the breach of them.

After another canter over the now well-trodden ground of the Irish plot, the Lord Chief Justice ended with the pious hope that the prisoner, now so near his end, would have the grace to repent of his false religion before it was too late.

### PLUNKETT:

May it please your lordship to give me leave to speak one word. If I were a man that had no care of my conscience in this matter, and did not think of God Almighty or conscience or heaven or hell, I might have saved my life; for I was offered it by divers people here, so I would but confess my own guilt and accuse others. But, my lord, I had rather die ten thousand deaths than wrongfully accuse anybody; and the time will come when your lordship will see what these witnesses are that have come in against me.

I do assure your lordship, if I were a man that had not good principles, I might easily have saved my life; but I had rather die ten thousand deaths, than wrongfully to take away one farthing of any man's goods, one day of his liberty, or one minute of his life.

**LORD CHIEF JUSTICE:**

I am sorry to see you persist in the principles of that religion.

**PLUNKETT:**

They are those principles that even God Almighty cannot dispense withal.

**LORD CHIEF JUSTICE:**

Well, however, the judgment which we must give you is that which the law says and speaks. And therefore you must go from hence to the place from whence you came, that is, to Newgate; and from thence you shall be drawn through the city of London to Tyburn; there you shall be hanged by the neck but cut down before you are dead, your bowels shall be taken out and burnt before your face, your head shall be cut off, and your body divided into four quarters, to be disposed of as his majesty pleases.

And I pray God to have mercy upon your soul.

A few formalities remained. The Court was graciously pleased to allow the condemned man the company of his servant for his last few days on earth; he could also have visitors, as long as there was a warder present. His request for a priest was ignored.

## 12. THE MARTYR

The last two weeks of Oliver's life were to prove a period of great happiness and peace. All the cares that had been his daily lot for so many years could now be set aside. He was visited by many of his friends and by some of the leading English Catholics, who came to give comfort but instead received it.

It must have been during this time that the Irish painter, Garret Morphey, drew the sketch of him that has formed the basis of almost all subsequent portraits of the Archbishop. The sketch itself has vanished but several copies still exist of an engraving made from it by the Dutch artist, Van der Vaart. It shows a man who looks older than his fifty-five years, with beard and moustache and shoulder-length white hair. The face is lined and worn but it has an expression of great dignity and strength about it. There is an almost other-worldly quality in the levelled eyes, which look without curiosity upon a world that is no longer of anything more than passing interest.

During these last few days he had the company of his servant and friend, James McKenna, who besides attending on him, also carried letters back and forth between him and his fellow-prisoner, Father Corker. Afterwards Corker described the Archbishop as he then appeared:

> The trial being ended and he condemned, his man had leave to wait on him alone in his chamber, by whose means we had free inter-course by letters to each other. And now it was I clearly perceived the Spirit of God in him, and those lovely fruits of the Holy Ghost, charity, joy, peace, patience, etc., transparent in his soul. And not only I, but many other Catholics who came to receive his benediction and were eye witnesses (a favour not denied to us) can testify.
>
> There appeared in his words, in his actions, in his very countenance, something so divinely elevated, such a composed mixture of cheerful-ness, constancy, courage, love, sweetness and candour, as manifestly denoted the divine good-ness had made him fit for a victim and destined him for heaven. None saw or came near him but received new comfort, new fervour, new desires to please, serve and suffer for Christ Jesus, by his very presence.

Among the letters he wrote at this time must have been several to his family. One survives, a letter written in English to Michael Plunkett, a relative of his who was studying in the Irish College, Rome. It survives because Michael left it in the Roman archives to be preserved for posterity. Writing to Michael, Oliver must have remembered his own student days in Rome and that prospect of martyrdom that attracted and repelled him at the same time; now he suddenly realises that death no longer holds any fear for him.

Sentence of death passed against me on 15th, without causing me any fear or depriving me of sleep for a quarter of an hour. I am innocent of all treason as the child born yesterday. As for my character, profession, and function, I did own it publicly, and that being also a motive of my death I die most willingly; and being the first among the Irish, I will teach others with the grace of God, by example, not to fear death. But how am I, a poor creature, so stout, seeing that my Redeemer began to fear, to be weary and sad, and that drops of his blood ran down to the ground? I have considered that Christ, by his fears and passions, merited for me to be without fear. . . .

I have recommended you to my friends there, and also my nephews and two nieces. Jemmy and Joseph begun their philosophy and Mickey ended his prosody. Catty and Tomasina and all will be in a sad condition. You know that Ned is simple, and that by Cromwell's people what little land and mortgages he had left him by his father were lost; and I believe my friends there will help my nephews, if you speak to Monsignore.

The letters he wrote to his fellow-prisoner, Father Corker, have also been preserved and they almost form a diary of those days. The first of them seems to have been written the day after his sentence.

Dear Sir,

I am obliged to you for the favour and charity of the £20 and for all your former benevolence, and whereas I cannot in this country remunerate you, with God's grace I hope to be grateful in that kingdom which is properly our country. And truly God gave me, though unworthy of it, that grace to have *fortem animam mortis terrore carentem.* *

I have many sins to answer for before the supreme Judge of the high bench where no false witnesses can have audience; but as for the bench yesterday, I am not guilty of any crime there objected to me. I would I could be so clear at the bench of the All-powerful, *ut ut sit.* †

There is one comfort, that he cannot be deceived because he is omniscious, and knows all secrets even of hearts, and cannot deceive because he is all goodness; so that I may be sure of a fair trial and will get time sufficient to call witnesses, nay, the Judge will bring them in a moment if there will be need of any.

You and your comrades' prayers will be powerful advocates at that bench (here none are admitted) for
    Your affectionate friend,

                Oliver Plunkett.

Two days later, on the 18th of June, he wrote about some money that had been received from another benefactor; evidently he was becoming a little overwhelmed by his visitors, as the last

---

* A valiant soul without fear of death.
† However it may be.

sentence shows: "I am informed the execution will be upon Tuesday; and I long to be out of all affairs, and to have one full day and night to recollect myself." A day or two later, he has still not completely overcome these distractions: "Oh, if I could but feel one act of true and lively contrition, I would be well satisfied. I often endeavour, but still I find some earthly thought do obstruct and hinder my good inspiration. . . . The passage is but short, yet 'tis dangerous, from time to eternity. It can never be repassed or reiterated. Your prayers I say I beg and your brethren's."

On the 23rd a new, and this time definite, date was set for his execution. "The Captain sent to me Mr Cooper to tell me that tomorrow sennight the execution will be. Whereas 'tis not upon St John's day, I am glad 'tis to be upon his octave and upon a Friday also. He tells me I will be allowed a priest. I desired it should be you. If it will be a person unknown to me, I intend to discourse but little with him."

The next day, the Feast of St John the Baptist, brought an unusually long letter. Oliver speaks with pride of the constancy of his brother bishops. "They might have saved their lives by going overseas, but the Irish prelates are resolved rather to die than to forsake their flocks. Forristal Kildariensis had departed but that I hindered him, for if the captains will fly, 'tis in vain to exhort the single soldiers to stand in battle. . . . By our deaths the number of Catholics will not be diminished but rather augmented, when they see we willingly die and contemn life, which is the only idol of our adversaries." Then he goes on to reflect on John the Baptist, who was beheaded in spite of his stainless life.

> He had not even venials and suffered prison and death; we have dunghills of mortals and what ought we to suffer? But why should I speak of St John, whereas his Master, who was free from all original, venial and actual sins, suffered cold, frost, hunger, prison, stripes, thorns, and the most painful death of the cross for others' sins, which death of the cross compared to that of Tyburn, as I hear the description of it, is but a flea-biting.*
>
> I ought therefore cheerfully desire it, heartily covet it, and joyfully embrace it, it being a sure way, a smooth path by which I may in a very short time pass from sorrow to joy, from toil to rest, and from a momentary time or duration to never-ending eternity.

If the Archbishop was troubled about his sins, his mind was soon set at rest. A day or so after this letter, Father Corker finally succeeded in gaining admission for a short while to Oliver's cell. They heard one another's confessions, gave and received absolution, and promised each other the support of their prayers. Furthermore, the requisites for Mass were brought to the cell, and Oliver had the happiness of celebrating the Eucharist daily for the last week of his life, including the day of his death.

The last seven days of Oliver's life marked the

* In his haste, Oliver has put this the wrong way round. He obviously means that Tyburn is but a fleabite compared to the cross.

last stage in his spiritual journey. It has been said that self-will dies a quarter of an hour after we do. During his final week on earth, Oliver, who had given up everything else, now gave that up as well. Looking back on his past life, he must have seen one fault that seemed to run its roots deepest into his character. Sometimes it had taken on the appearance of a virtue: steadfastness, determination, single-mindedness. Other times it had showed its less attractive face: his friends had called it touchiness, his enemies had called it arrogance or high-handedness.

All his life he had been a fighter. When a thing had to be done, he did it regardless of the cost. When criticised for his actions, he had always answered his critics, point for point. He had never doubted that he was in the right. But even in the right, one can sometimes be wrong. The memory of those pathetic priests, his last accusers, was not easily shaken from his mind. He had disciplined them in the past, and justly; but could there have been a place for mercy that his self-righteousness did not see? Had his hardness helped to bring them to that sad pass? Had he given them some reason to hate him so much?

What thoughts went through Oliver's mind in that last week, after his one and only meeting with his priest-friend, we cannot fully know. We do know that, by a deliberate and conscious decision, he stripped himself completely of self-will and submitted totally to the will of another. That other was Father Maurus Corker.

Most of his remaining communications with

Corker concerned his speech from the scaffold. This was a matter of some importance, since it would be printed and widely circulated in London and elsewhere. A friend had written a draft for him but he did not like it because it was "too sharp against Parliament, Judges and Jury", a comment one would not have expected from him in former times. He then made out his own version which was shuttled back and forth between the two cells for Corker's suggestions and corrections; all his emendations, which were slight enough, were gratefully accepted.

Corker's description of him during these last few days is memorable.

After he certainly knew God Almighty had chosen him to the crown and dignity of martyrdom, he continually studied how to divest himself of himself, and become more and more an entire, pleasing and perfect holocaust. To which end, as he gave up his soul with all its faculties to the conduct of God, so for God's sake he resigned the care and disposal of his body to unworthy me, and this in such an absolute manner that he looked upon himself to have no further power or authority over it.

For an instance of this, the day before he suffered, when I sent a barber to trim him, the man asked him if he should leave anything on his upper lip. He answered he knew not how I would have it, and he would do nothing without my order, so that they were forced to send to me before the barber could finish his work.

Another remarkable instance of his strange humility and resignation was that, about an hour before he was carried to execution, being desired to drink a little glass of sack to strengthen his spirits, he answered he was not at his own disposal but mine, and that he must have leave from me before he would either take it or refuse it; whereupon, though I was locked up, yet for his satisfaction his man and the keeper's wife came to my chamber, and then returning back told him I enjoined it, upon which he readily submitted.

The strange incident of the glass of wine shows not only his submission to Corker's will, but his desire to follow his Master's example as closely as possible in his passion. He was evidently thinking of the Gospel account: "they brought him to the place called Golgotha (which means the place of a skull), and they offered him wine mingled with myrrh; but he did not take it" *(Mark 15:22-23)*.

His last letter to Corker was written on the eve of his death.

Sir,
I do most earnestly recommend myself to your prayers and to the most holy sacrifices of all the noble confessors who are in this prison and to such priests as you are acquainted with; and I hope soon to be able to requite all your and their kindness. Above all I recommend myself to the prayers of the holy families of Mr Sheldon and the Lady Staffords, and in general to all the good Catholics in this city whose faith and charity are great.

I do recommend to you and to them my most faithful servant, James McKenna, who served me these eleven years. Some of the good Catholics who came to see me told me that after my death they would be charitable to him.

I desire that you be pleased to tell all my benefactors that for all eternity I will be mindful of them, and that I will pray for them until they will come where I hope to come soon, and then also will thank them *in conspectu supremi Domini.* * They deserve all praise in this and, by God's grace, a crown of glory in the next.

I doubt not but their faith, charity and good works will be efficacious with our Saviour, and that there will soon be an end of this persecution and that *iniquitas multorum mox revelabitur. Fiat voluntas Dei, fiat, fiat.*† And I beseech my Saviour to give all the good Catholics perseverance in their faith and good works and to grant me the grace to be tomorrow where I may pray for them *non in aenigmate* but *facie ad faciem* etc. ††

And be sure that I am and still will be,

Your obliged friend,
Oliver Plunkett.

On the night before his death, the Archbishop went to bed at eleven o'clock and slept quite soundly until four the next morning, when he was awakened by McKenna who had slept in the cell with him. He rose and said his last Mass, with McKenna as his server. Then he dealt with a few items of unfinished business and scribbled a couple

---

* In the sight of the most high Lord.
† The iniquity of many will soon be revealed. God's will be done.
†† Not in darkness but face to face.

of last-minute messages for Father Corker; though
the word "scribbled" is not altogether appropriate,
for the writing is firm and clear. Then, as we have
seen, he drank a glass of sack and waited for the
summons from the prison governor.

Oliver was to have a companion in his suffering
that day. He was Edward Fitzharris, an unfortunate informer who had misjudged his perjuries
and had been caught in the trap he had set for
others. He had been sentenced to death on the
same day as Oliver and then returned to his prison
in the Tower of London.

An execution was an elaborate affair in those
days and the procession to Tyburn was an important part of the spectacle. On that morning of the
1st of July, the cavalry and foot-soldiers assembled
at the Tower between eight and nine, while
Fitzharris was brought out and put lying on the
sledge, a kind of wooden boat dragged along the
ground by horses. Then the procession formed and
moved off through the crowds in the direction of
Newgate.

In Newgate, Oliver was taken from his cell and
laid on a second sledge in the press-yard. When
asked by the Lieutenant of the Tower how the
Archbishop had borne himself, the Governor of
Newgate is said to have replied: "Very well, for
when I came to him this morning, he was newly
awake, having slept all night without any disturbance; and when I told him to prepare for his
execution, he received the message with all quietness of mind, and went to the sledge as unconcerned as if he had been going to a wedding." The

procession re-formed itself around the two condemned men and continued on to Tyburn, a
distance of about two miles.

At Tyburn they halted in front of the great
gallows, where twenty men could hang at a time.
Fitzharris, terrified, had to be helped to the
gallows, where he retracted everything he had said
at his trial and accused Shaftesbury's agents of
having suborned him. The Archbishop, by contrast,
was perfectly calm as he delivered his prepared
speech to the attentive and unexpectedly sympathetic crowd.

He began by detailing the charges that had been
made against him under seven heads, and answered
each one separately, before going on to a general
protestation of his innocence and of the absurdity
of the charges to anyone who knew the Irish
situation. "I dare mention farther and affirm, that
if these points of seventy thousand men, etc. had
been sworn before any Protestant jury in Ireland
and had been even acknowledged by me at the bar,
they would not believe me, no more than if it had
been deposed and confessed by me that I had
flown in the air from Dublin to Holyhead."

He then went on to speak of the false witnesses
and particularly of the four priests who had
testified against him, "which wicked act, being a
defect of persons, ought not to reflect on the
Order of St Francis or on the Roman Catholic
clergy, it being well known that there was a Judas
among the twelve apostles and a wicked man,
called Nicholas, amongst the seven deacons."

I do heartily forgive them, and also the judges, who by denying me sufficient time to bring my records and witnesses from Ireland did expose my life to evident danger. I do also forgive all those who had a hand in bringing me from Ireland to be tried here, where it was morally impossible for me to have a fair trial. I do finally forgive all who did concur directly or indirectly to take away my life; and I ask forgiveness of all those whom I ever offended by thought, word or deed. I beseech the All-powerful that his divine majesty grant the King, the Queen, and the Duke of York, and all the royal family, health, long life and all prosperity in this world, and in the next everlasting felicity.

Now that I have shown sufficiently, as I think, how innocent I am of any plot or conspiracy, I would I were able with the like truth to clear myself of high crimes committed against the divine majesty's commandments, often transgressed by me, for which I am sorry with all my heart; and if I should or could live a thousand years I have a firm resolution and a strong purpose by your grace, O my God, never to offend you. And I beseech your divine majesty, by the merits of Christ and by the intercession of his Blessed Mother and all the holy angels and saints, to forgive me my sins and to grant my soul eternal rest.

Having finished his speech, the Archbishop stood quietly reciting some prayers in Latin while the hangman adjusted the nooses around his neck and the neck of his companion and pulled woollen caps down over their faces. The platform on which they were standing was a cart, drawn by a horse. Three priests hidden in the crowd pronounced the words of absolution as the horse was driven forward and the two men were left dangling from the high gallows beam.

Nearby was the quartering block, with knives and cleavers for the dismembering. Since the hangman was accustomed to use his victims in accordance with the sympathy or otherwise of the crowd, it is likely that the Archbishop was unconscious and perhaps even dead when he was cut down and the butchering began.

A report sent to Rome shortly after his death, probably by an English Jesuit, made this comment:

All write with one accord that this innocent victim has done and yet performs great good in England, not only by the edification which he gave to the Catholics, but moreover by the change of ideas and sentiments which he occasioned in many Protestants, who now commence to regard all these conspiracies as malicious fictions; and there are great grounds for believing that the fruit which England will derive from his blood will not end here.

The prophecy was quickly shown to be true. The 1st of July was the day when the people of England finally turned against the Popish Plot and its makers. Next morning the Earl of Shaftesbury was arrested and lodged in the Tower of London. Oliver Plunkett was the last man to be martyred for the Catholic faith in England.

## 13. THE SAINT

The news of Oliver Plunkett's appointment as Archbishop of Armagh did not meet with universal approval among his fellow-countrymen; neither did the news of his canonisation. For three hundred years he has continued to be a controversial figure in Irish history.

There is a saying, popular in Ireland, to the effect that there is no smoke without a fire. On that principle, many people have felt that there must have been some fundamental flaw in the Archbishop's character to have drawn so much obloquy, some sinister secret still under wraps in the inmost recesses of the Vatican archives. Yet there is another saying that may be more apposite, namely, that if you throw enough mud, some of it is bound to stick. The fact that his reputation remains vaguely tarnished to this day may be attributable to the vigour and persistence of the mud-slingers rather than to the accuracy of their aim.

When a man is declared a saint, it does not mean that all his actions have been canonised. There are some saints who seem always to have been saints, from the cradle to the grave. There are others who became saints by a sudden act of conversion, turning from a life of sin to a life of holiness. And there are others again who achieved sainthood by a lifelong process of growth, grace building upon nature, which only reached its fullness with the end of life itself. St Peter, most unrocklike of rocks, was one of those. Oliver Plunkett was another.

It is not that he was ever anything less than a good man, a devout priest, and a holy archbishop. When we examine the accusations against him, they are hard to substantiate. The allegations of unchastity boil down to the two months' career of Captain Brown, an episode which a modern generation finds endearing rather than shocking. The Oliver of the singing pubs may never make the stained-glass windows but he shows a humanity and enterprise that disarms criticism.

The charge that he showed a certain lack of courage when he chose Rome in preference to Ireland may have a little more basis in fact. At the same time, an excessive desire for martyrdom is unhealthy: it is something to be accepted when offered, not something to be sought. It is true that he stayed in Rome when persecution raged and returned when it had stopped, but it is equally true that he stayed on in Ireland when the persecution was renewed and when he might have chosen exile without too much dishonour. It is impossible to underestimate the importance of that decision for the Irish Church in an age when absentee bishops were common even in the peaceful countries of

Southern Europe. By word and example he hammered home the principle that a bishop's place was with his people, that a bishopric was a service to be rendered rather than a benefice to be enjoyed, that it was sheer hypocrisy to exhort the private soldiers to stand if the captains fled. If that was something that later generations in Ireland came to take for granted, it was only because he upheld it at the cost of his life.

The most serious accusation against him and the one that has persisted longest is that he was high-handed and autocratic in his dealings with his clergy. We have already seen how John Brennan found him touchy and hot-tempered in his dispute with the Archbishop of Dublin in 1672. In his great philippic of 1679 Friar Anthony Daly went a good deal further. "The Primate, acting in a manner that can only be called Machiavellian, seems to think that he cannot rule his subjects properly unless he divides them into factions and then treats these with alternate favour and disfavour. . . . There is no diocese in Ulster that he has not deprived of its Vicar-Generals, scarcely any parish where he has not deposed the parish priest to the scandal of the clergy and people." Allowing for the hyperbole, it is still true that Oliver's relations with the clergy were often stormy and acrimonious and that he felt called upon to use his powers of suspension and deposition with some regularity.

Was he a Counter-Reformation bigot and bully, ready to fire all his artillery at the first hint of disobedience? Or did he find himself faced with a critical situation which could only be dealt with by the most drastic measures? The evidence suggests that the second reading is the truer one, that discipline among the clergy had broken down to such an extent that the very existence of the Church was threatened. The collapse of the Catholic Church in England around this period is attributed by historians to the fact that there were no resident bishops to give firm leadership and put an end to the constant squabbling among the clergy.

Whether Oliver acted justly in individual instances can be judged only by examining the individual instances; and in most cases it is no longer possible to do so. We know there were times when he treated delinquent priests with great kindness, among them the Franciscans Harold and Coppinger and the Augustinian French. In other cases he acted more harshly, with what justification we cannot now judge. The clergy have their rights, but so have the laity. When the local parish priest is supporting himself and his houseful of illegitimate children by means of highway robbery, something more than a disapproving silence is called for. If his way of acting was autocratic, it may also have been necessary; and it was certainly courageous, for he knew well the risks he was running in tangling with some of these men.

*Finis coronat opus*, as Oliver with his liking for Latin tags might well have remarked: the ending crowns the work. For him it proved to be a long-drawn-out ending: almost a year in Dublin Castle, another eight months in Newgate of which six were spent in solitary confinement, before the final ordeal. For at least twelve of those nineteen months he lived in the constant expectation of a cruel and violent death.

That imprisonment and especially that extraordinary half year in the solitary cell, when in the cold and darkness of winter he fasted even from the scanty prison food for three days a week and spent his time in continuous prayer, was his greatest test and his greatest victory. All that was good in him was strengthened and intensified, all that was unruly was brought into obedience. His will was led to that perfect conformity with the will of God which is the essence of sainthood.

Without those last nineteen months we might remember him as a devoted and courageous churchman and nothing more. But those months were as much a part of his life as anything that went before; in the divine plan, they were the time given him for the final perfecting of his great soul. The noose that closed around his neck at Tyburn made him a martyr. The life that prepared him for that noose had already made him a saint.

# NOTES AND ACKNOWLEDGEMENTS

The eagerly awaited edition of Oliver Plunkett's letters by Mgr John Hanly was regrettably not yet available at the time this book was written. The text of the Roman letters is therefore mainly from the versions given in Cardinal Moran's *Memoir of Oliver Plunket*, though the translation has been modernised. The English letters are taken from the printed versions given in *The Downside Review* of 1921, but with spelling and punctuation brought up to date. The text of the Irish verses is taken from *Dánfhocail*, edited by Thomas F. O'Rahilly.

A special word of acknowledgement is due to Father Tomás Ó Fiaich and Father Benignus Millet, O.F.M., for their generous assistance and for providing some quotations which do not appear to have been published before, notably those on pages 59 and 77.

In the seventeenth century, England and Ireland used the Old Style Calendar which was ten days behind that used in most other parts of Europe. Thus the date of Oliver Plunkett's death, the 1st of July, corresponds to the 11th of July in modern reckoning.